Praise for *Spells from Scratch*

"Phoenix Silverstar defines a spell as 'a mechanism for making the possible probable.' 'Remember,' she says, 'magic is not miracles.' Primarily but not exclusively designed for Wiccans, *Spells from Scratch* is a comprehensive grimoire addressing all aspects of spellcraft, from ethics to elements. Detailed instructions, correspondences, ingredients, incantations, and examples are provided to craft effective spells for every need: healing, transformation, protection, love, and beauty. A valuable addition to any magickal library."

—Oberon Zell, author of *Grimoire for the Apprentice Wizard* and headmaster of Grey School of Wizardry

"This book covers the basics and more; it is perfect for the beginner. If you have been practicing for years, there are some new tricks that you can pick up. It is easy to read and understand; she presents the material well. I highly recommend this book. It needs to be in your library."

—Tish Owen, author of *Spell it Correctly*

T0050047

SPELLS FROM SCRATCH

About the Author

Phoenix Silverstar is a member of the Aquarian Tabernacle Church and former Dean of Faculty and teacher at the Woolston-Steen Theological Seminary, having retired at the end of 2021. She is a long-time practitioner of magic and also shares her knowledge of magic, mythology, and other subjects as a presenter at events and festivals everywhere.

To Write to the Author

If you wish to contact the author or would like more information about this book, please write to the author in care of Llewellyn Worldwide Ltd. and we will forward your request. Both the author and publisher appreciate hearing from you and learning of your enjoyment of this book and how it has helped you. Llewellyn Worldwide Ltd. cannot guarantee that every letter written to the author can be answered, but all will be forwarded. Please write to:

Phoenix Silverstar
℅ Llewellyn Worldwide
2143 Wooddale Drive
Woodbury, MN 55125-2989

Please enclose a self-addressed stamped envelope for reply,
or $1.00 to cover costs. If outside the U.S.A., enclose
an international postal reply coupon.

Many of Llewellyn's authors have websites with additional information and resources. For more information, please visit our website at http://www.llewellyn.com.

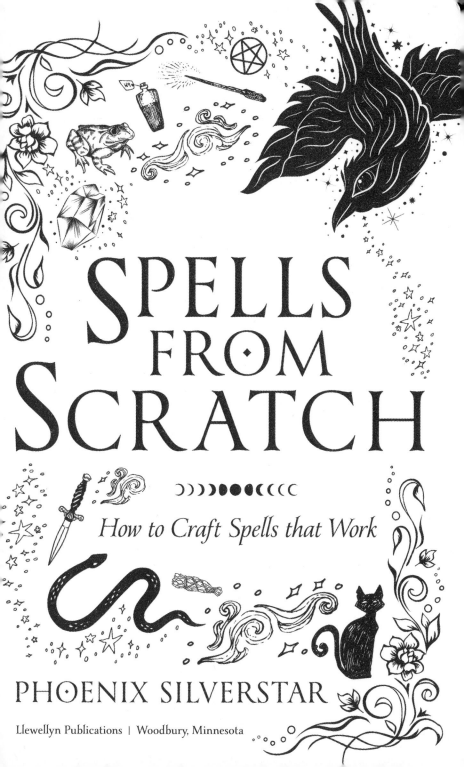

SPELLS FROM SCRATCH

))))●●●●(((

How to Craft Spells that Work

PHOENIX SILVERSTAR

Llewellyn Publications | Woodbury, Minnesota

FIRST EDITION
First Printing, 2022

Book design by Samantha Peterson
Cover design by Cassie Willett
Interior art by Llewellyn Art Department

Llewellyn Publications is a registered trademark of Llewellyn Worldwide Ltd.

Library of Congress Cataloging-in-Publication Data (Pending)
ISBN: 978-0-7387-6983-7

Llewellyn Worldwide Ltd. does not participate in, endorse, or have any authority or responsibility concerning private business transactions between our authors and the public.

All mail addressed to the author is forwarded but the publisher cannot, unless specifically instructed by the author, give out an address or phone number.

Any internet references contained in this work are current at publication time, but the publisher cannot guarantee that a specific location will continue to be maintained. Please refer to the publisher's website for links to authors' websites and other sources.

Llewellyn Publications
A Division of Llewellyn Worldwide Ltd.
2143 Wooddale Drive
Woodbury, MN 55125-2989
www.llewellyn.com

Printed in the United States of America

CONTENTS

Contents

PART FOUR: SPELLS FOR EVERY NEED

DISCLAIMER

This book is presented solely for educational and entertainment purposes. The author and publisher are not offering it as medical advice. For diagnosis or treatment of any medical condition, readers are advised to consult or seek the services of a competent medical professional.

While best efforts have been used in preparing this book, the author and publisher make no representations or warranties of any kind. Neither the author nor the publisher shall be held liable or responsible to any person or entity with respect to any loss or damages caused, or alleged to have been caused, directly or indirectly, by the information contained herein. Every situation is different, and the advice and strategies contained herein may not be suitable for your situation.

Disclaimer

In the following pages, you will find recommendations for the use of certain herbs, essential oils, incense blends, and ritual items. If you are allergic to any of these items, please refrain from use. Each body reacts differently to herbs, essential oils, and other items, so results may vary from person to person. Essential oils are potent; use care when handling them. Always dilute essential oils before placing them on your skin, and make sure to do a patch test on your skin before use. Perform your own research before using an essential oil. Some herbal remedies can react with prescription or over-the-counter medications in adverse ways. Please do not ingest any herbs if you aren't sure you have identified them correctly. If you are on medication or have health issues, please do not ingest any herbs without first consulting a qualified practitioner.

ACKNOWLEDGMENTS

There are very many people with whom I have discussed the topics covered in this volume, and I am grateful to each and every one of you. No one named and no one forgotten.

The Woolston-Steen Theological Seminary faculty members all have influenced my thinking on many magical topics, and I much appreciate the effort, deep thought, and enthusiasm that they put into their work.

I wish especially to thank KerrO'Wen, who convinced me to pick up and finish writing this book when it had gone dormant due to too many priorities being juggled, and then cheered me on through to the finish.

This was not anywhere near the book it is now before the inputs of the fantastic editing staff at Llewellyn, especially Heather Greene and Nicole Borneman. My heartfelt thanks, Heather and Nicole!

INTRODUCTION

Magic is not miracles. Magic is making the possible probable.

When first thinking of using magic, most people want to go the easy way, so they buy a spell book full of spells written by someone else or purchase spell kits with ready-made incantations and items to use in the spell. Depending on the skill of the person who crafted the spells and how well you execute them, such spells may or may not be effective for you.

Maybe you are already practicing magic, but your magic is not working right. Perhaps you use cookbook formulas, but you do not understand how they work. Or you may already be working magic just fine, but you could use some inspiration for new spells. In any case, once you have finished reading this book, you will know how to create your own powerful spells from scratch, and if you are already a seasoned spell-crafter, you will have found new inspiration.

In this book, you will gain an understanding of what a spell is and isn't, the theory behind how to create spells, when to do magic and when not to, the importance of Acting in Accord, and how to manifest your goal. You will also learn some valuable symbols for spell work, as well as some magical correspondences and why you may want to use them. You will learn to write your own incantations, and I will provide specific spells as examples of the methods presented.

This book you hold in your hands is not a cookbook of ready-made spells. Instead, it teaches you how spells work and how to create spells for yourself, for your specific intents and purposes. It teaches you how to Act in Accord to manifest your goals. This is powerful magic. This is magic that works!

I like to think of my magic work as "spells without hocus pocus." This refers to the fact that some grimoires and old spell books are filled with incantations that contain mysterious words, e.g., names of spirits and beings about whom you know little or nothing. A great example of this is a thirteenth-century spell for healing by Albertus Magnus, which uses the incantation:

))))●●●((((

Ofano, Oblamo, Ospergo

Hola Noa Massa

Lux, Beff, Cletemati, Adonai

Cleona, Florit.

Pax Sax Sarax.

Afa Afca Nostra.

Cerum, Heaium, Lada Frium[1]

))))●●●((((

---

1. Gaynor, *Witchcraft Collection Volume Two*, chap. M.

I do not know what this means, nor do most people, as far as I know. What I do know is that it could very well backfire! Sending out intent when you do not know what it is may be useless and is also potentially dangerous.

What you are reading now, on the other hand, strives to leave nothing unexplained. The goal is for you, the reader, to understand the underlying mechanics of spell work so that you yourself become proficient in writing spells, so you are no longer forced to rely on the sometimes-dubious work of others. You will be able to write spells specific to your exact wants and needs, and you'll know all the necessary steps to take to make them manifest. You do not need to worry about whether the person who wrote the spell knew what they were doing, because you will know what you are doing. Knowing this puts all the power in your hands.

Magic is not an inherited skill or something into which you need to be born. Anyone can learn to cast spells! Once you have learned the steps required to create a spell, understand how to plan for the best timing, and know how to use correspondences and other tools that power your magic, you have all the necessary knowledge. All you need to add is the focus and intensity of emotion that is required.

This book also contains examples of complete spells, all written according to the principles explained here. You may use these as they appear here if you so choose. However, my real intent was to include them to illustrate the principles with actual examples so that you understand how to create your own spell.

You will find that some of the material in this book is written in a Wiccan context, draws on Wiccan principles, or has Wiccan references. This is not, however, an "introduction to Wicca" textbook, and you do not have to be Wiccan to learn the spell craft presented here. I am a third-degree British Traditional Wicca High Priestess, and that is why there are the occasional Wiccan flavors. Wicca is a religion that honors both the feminine and the masculine in the Divine, and thus you will find both Gods and Goddesses discussed. Incidentally, today many Wiccans also honor the entire gender spectrum in the same way. Many Wiccans also perform spells as part of their religious practice, as I do. In my case, I started doing magic and manifesting my intents in my teens, long before becoming a Wiccan in 2003.

My life experiences have influenced my spell work. I have been traveling to India regularly since 1986, when I married into an Indian Hindu family. I also lived in India for nine years. There, I was immersed in the culture and religion of Hinduism and the worship of Hindu deities. Thus, there are some Indian cultural concepts and Hindu religious concepts included among the principles. For example, one way that living in India has influenced my Witchcraft is that I incorporate the chakra system into my magic.

Similarly, I have a strong connection with the Norse Old Gods and myths because I was born and raised in Sweden. As a child, when we studied the Norse Æsir and the Vanir Gods in school, I was fascinated and always wondered how the belief in the Old Gods came to be entirely eliminated. As I grew older, I started working with these Gods as part of religious magic, a concept that will be explained in detail later on.

It is my hope that on every single page, you will find something that you can use in your own magical workings. I have often been frustrated by books that purport to teach a subject but turn out mostly to be a lot of words with little substance. In such books, you have to hunt and peck for any information that is actually useful in practice. My aim and hope here are that you will have a very different experience with this book, one where you find yourself thinking *Oh! I can use this! Oh, this is useful!* as you read through the chapters.

Part One

))))●●●(((

GETTING
STARTED

Chapter 1

))) ●●●(((

WHAT IS A SPELL?

When you hear someone talk about spells, you might picture a witch in sweeping black or purple robes standing with a wand in her hand, reading from an aged leather-bound book and mumbling a long incantation of mysterious words over a bubbling cauldron. You might see the room as lit only by candles; maybe a fire in the fireplace. Her black cat is by her side as she casts her spell…This beautiful setting, of course, happens, and yet this is not the way most spell workers cast spells. First of all, witches are of any gender. Rather than spells being cast in the enticing metaphysical setting that is often pictured, it is considerably more common to cast spells in much more mundane surroundings. The content of the spell and the words of the incantation are what is important. As you have already learned, the words should be clear and precise rather than mysterious.

Some of the most powerful spells are created specifically for the situation and the purpose of the spell, and that is precisely why they have so much power. These spells are tailored to the exact conditions at hand and the specific goal that the spell worker wants to manifest. They possess the personal power of the practitioner and are personalized to their exact needs. These spells cannot be found in spell books, where you will only find relatively generic spells. Some spells you may create at the spur-of-the-moment, e.g., adding love to a meal while cooking it or saying a spell of protection when the airplane you are in hits some turbulence. Other spells are carefully crafted, using many layers of symbols and correspondences, and executed at specific times in the lunar cycle, astrological configurations, and planetary hours. Again, these types of spells will not be found in a book of prewritten spells.

Here is my definition of a spell: a spell is a mechanism for making the possible probable. Remember, magic is not miracles.

In order to be successful, what you wish to manifest must first be created on the astral plane. You will learn how to do this later in this chapter. You will also learn what is required for a spell to work and what often causes magic to fail.

The Planes of Existence

There are many planes in our existence. This book will be concerned with the physical plane, where you experience mundane life, and where a chair is a chair that you can touch and feel, and also with the astral plane, where all consciousness and universal unconsciousness resides, and where a chair is a chair that only the astral body can move.

In order for anything to manifest on the physical plane, it must first exist on the astral plane. Some things come into existence on the astral plane all on their own, based on the will of deity or probabilistic rules, just like on the physical plane. Others, you create deliberately so that they can manifest in the physical plane. Creating on the astral plane is somewhat like creating the blueprint for the physical goal.

When you have a particular goal that you wish to manifest in the physical, you therefore first create it in the astral. You create it in the astral through spell work, including visualizing in the astral the goal as already being manifest and adding all the emotions you feel about manifesting your dream. You tell the Universe how it is, and the Universe nods and adjusts so that it is so. The approach works because our personal cosmos in the brain is a microcosm that mirrors and is mirrored by the macrocosm. As above, so below. As within, so without.

Some practitioners view the Universe as a web and see a spell as pulling some threads toward you from the web, weaving them into the pattern you want to manifest, and then putting that pattern back into the web. All are valid ways of expressing the same concept.

For it to be possible for the goal to manifest from its existence in the astral to the physical plane, you need to send the energy of the spell to the time and place where this needs to happen. If you are a group, you do so by chanting an incantation, singing, dancing, drumming, etc., and then the group releases the energy together to where and when it needs to be.

When you work alone, you can raise energy in several ways (described in chapter 7). Then you send that energy to the time and place it needs to be by pushing it to where you visualize the goal as being manifest in the physical. Sometimes you push the energy all at once. Sometimes you put the energy into a spell object and let the magic release over time.

To give a spell additional power, you can do something called magic layering. To do this, you need to know and use the laws of magic. Before you go there, please read the rules that will keep you safe and make your magic more powerful.

The Astral Temple

If you do not already have an astral temple where you can work in peace, build one now. An astral temple is a temple you create on the astral plane, the nonphysical realm where our consciousness, knowledge, wisdom, and thought reside. You can do spell work in the astral temple if it is impossible for you to do so on the physical level. You can also go to your astral temple just to relax. It is a place for your mind to do work or to rest.

Exercise: The Astral Temple

You will need

A quiet spot where you can sit comfortably and undisturbed

A pen and paper to write some notes at the end (optional)

Close your eyes and think of what makes you feel at complete peace. The place should make your shoulders relax and come down. Your tongue should not be pressed hard to the roof of your mouth, and you should feel all tension leave your body. You should feel at peace with the world.

Once you have found this place of relaxation, begin to envision your astral temple. If you need help, use the following questions to deepen your connection to your astral temple.

- What sort of environment am I in? Am I deep in a forest, on a beach, or in a high-ceilinged building? On a boat? In a clearing? Is there a building of some sort?
- What does it look like?
- What does it smell like?
- Are there sounds?
- Is there a breeze on your skin?
- Does the air have a taste?
- Are there symbols?
- Is there a deity that lives here?
- Are there decorations?

Be as detailed as you can while creating your astral temple. Remember that this is not a physical temple, so you can be as elaborate as you wish. Mine has floor-length silk chiffon curtains fluttering in the breeze, pearl-and-gemstone inlaid marble wall decorations behind the altar, and gold pitchers, among other luxuries. Your temple may change over time, or this may be the temple that will be yours for the rest of your life.

Be certain to find in your astral temple an area (or several) where you can work with the goals you want to manifest. This can be your main astral altar, an altar that you dedicate to manifestation, a grove in the forest, or any setting that you feel is suitable for this type of magic. If you already have an astral temple, go there now and find where you will work with the next goal that you wish to manifest in the physical.

Chapter 1

Reasons for Spell Success or Failure

Spells are not guaranteed to work. Spells can fail for a myriad of reasons. The most common cause of failure is that the practitioner lost faith in their ability to manifest that goal. Questioning and being uncertain immediately sends out signals to the Universe that the goal is in doubt. Always watch your thoughts!

Another common reason for failure is lack of engagement when casting the spell. You need to be 100 percent engaged intellectually and emotionally for the spell to take hold. If your mind is wandering, the spell gets attenuated, and nothing much is likely to happen as a result. Grounding and centering before casting a spell is always a good idea.

The final reason for a spell not working is making no provisions for it to work. The Universe cannot make the impossible happen. You need to make your goal possible so that magic can make it probable. (More about that under "Acting in Accord.")

Don't Block Your Magic Unintentionally: The Power of Thought

As you go about your day, you think many thoughts. These go out to the Universe like miniature Thoughtforms and mostly dissolve into the cacophony of thoughts from people all over the world. No effect comes out of that. If, however, you keep thinking the same thing over and over, you are unintentionally establishing in the astral whatever it is that you are thinking. This is a good thing if you are thinking productive and positive thoughts. Often, though, thoughts are far from productive and positive. They can be negative and outright destructive. When this happens, you are sabotaging your magic. When you have worked hard on a spell to establish a desired outcome in the astral, then if you doubt that it will come to pass or think that something different will happen, you are tearing down what you went to so much trouble to create. In addition, your thoughts affect your emotions, and your emotions affect your behavior and actions. Your behavior and actions affect the outcome. In the case of a spell, if you think negative thoughts about the goal you want to manifest, you will feel sad and unsure about the outcome, and you are inadvertently putting barriers in place for Acting in Accord. Your behavior has changed through the emotions stemming from your thoughts of doubt.

On the other hand, if you always tell yourself that you will manifest your goal, you add substance to what you already built in the astral. Furthermore, you feel buoyed by your thoughts, and therefore you are significantly more likely to go through with your plan of action for Acting in Accord. This is why you must have absolute confidence that your magic works.

Bringing Back Belief in Magic

Children have an innate understanding of the fact that their actions, thoughts, and words affect their reality. As they grow, adults keep telling them that this is fallacious "magical thinking," and their belief wanes. For magic to work, the practitioner must believe that it does. If the practitioner does not, the Universe hears doubt, and the spell will fizzle.

Given the general lack of belief in magic in society, it takes some extra effort to bring that childlike understanding of how magic works back. The first step is to realize that everything around you that is manufactured is the result of someone having an idea—a thought. A glass started with someone designing the shape of the glass. A carpet started with someone thinking, *I would like to weave a carpet. What design should I do?* These are very concrete examples of someone's thoughts having created a new reality, a reality with a new glass or a new carpet in it. How you choose to dress and how you act are reflections of your thoughts about yourself. As within, so without. This turns out to be a circle that feeds itself. If you think poorly of yourself, you will dress poorly and act poorly. If you make an active decision to dress better and be more kind, you will find that it affects how you think of yourself!

Thus, you must be clear about what needs to be accomplished for the magic to work, but that is not sufficient. You must also have a great desire to achieve this goal, a strong drive. Your emotions when performing the spell add a tremendous amount of power to the magic and propel you to Act in Accord.

When your thoughts and emotions are synchronized around what you want to accomplish, you send powerful signals both to the Universe and to your own subconscious. Your thoughts come from your conscious mind and send signals to your subconscious mind, where your emotions originate and from where they emanate. These two, in tandem, constitute your magical power.

That is, however, still not enough. You must believe. The people who are healed at healing springs or other sacred healing sites have three things in common: they can clearly see their lives as if they were healed; they come with a strong desire to be healed; they believe in the power of the healing site to be able to heal them. They believe that they will be healed. Then—magic happens!

In terms of practicing magic, believing means to be confident without any hint of doubt that the outcome can and will materialize. By stating the outcome in present tense and as if it is already true, you are creating the understanding both in your conscious and unconscious minds that the outcome is attainable and real. At the same time, you are sending that conviction to the Universe to act accordingly. You can do this. It is your key to success.

Acting in Accord

Say that you want a new job, so when the moon is a waxing crescent, you perform a great spell, saying, "By the time the moon is dark again, I have a new full-time, permanent position with a company that offers medical and dental and other benefits that I am entitled to, and I earn at least $XYZ per month. I love my responsibilities; I am very capable of doing them, and I get along well with my coworkers and my boss. There is a career path ahead, and I am very happy with my job. For the greatest good of all, so mote it be." You visualize yourself working hard in your new job with a great, big, happy smile on your face. Then you go and turn on the TV, sit down in the comfy chair, and watch your favorite daytime show. You do this day after day, and when the dark moon comes around again, the phone has not rung with any job offers, you are still unemployed, and you are upset and start to doubt your magical abilities. The spell went wrong.

But remember, magic is not miracles. Magic is making the possible probable. By doing absolutely nothing and not actually looking for a position, you made it darn near impossible for the spell to work. What you missed doing is Acting in Accord.

The phrase is important. *Acting in Accord* means setting the stage so that the spell can work. It means making your goal possible so that the spell can then make it probable. In the example, it means polishing your resume, going to the store to get clothes that are appropriate for interviewing, maybe getting a haircut and a manicure, updating your LinkedIn if applicable and needed, and of course, sending in employment applications! Now, when the moon goes dark again, you are sitting at your desk in your new job, thrilled with your new position and confident in your magic. See the difference?

Whenever you cast a spell, also write a list of the steps that you need to take to enable the spell to work!

Exercise: Defining How to Act in Accord for a Goal

You will need

Pen and paper

Think of a goal you have in life. Then, write down the steps that you need to take to make it possible. Make sure that you start with small steps, including something you can do today to get started. Then go do it.

What Lies Ahead?

Now that we've reached the end of the first chapter, you are ready to learn the details of crafting a spell. You know that you need to create your goal in the astral plane, you know that you need to Act in Accord, and you will soon learn about the Law of Similarity, the Law of Contagion, and religious magic.

In the following few chapters, you will learn about symbols and how to choose them, as well as correspondences and how to use them. You will also learn how to place your goal manifestation at a particular point in the future. In fact, you will learn how to work every necessary part of a spell.

So, what are the parts of a spell that you need to think about?

- A well-formed goal—what is to be manifest
- The checklist for ensuring that the goal is sound
- Ethics check

- The time when the goal is to be reached, using a method described later
- The list of steps for Acting in Accord
- A set of correspondences for layering the spell, and where to get them or how to create them
- The deity or deities that will support the goal being manifest, if you will use religious magic
- Something from the person for whom you are working the spell
- The incantation
- When and where you will perform the spell
- A list of all the items that are going to be required to cast the spell (gather the items ahead of time, as having to stop in the middle of casting a spell to run to grab a needed item is very disruptive and interferes with your power)

Soon, you will be ready to put this all together and begin writing and performing spells.

Chapter 2

))))●●●(((C

ETHICS AND LAWS
⊙F MAGIC

Magic has parallels to natural sciences. There are laws of magic that create a cause-and-effect relationship. When you understand how these laws work, it puts you in control of potent magic.

Magic also has parallels to mundane legal and judicial systems. The ethics of magic define what you are allowed to do and what you are not allowed to do, just like laws do in mundane life. The Threefold Law can be likened to the mundane judicial system in that if you break the rules of ethics, the Threefold Law metes out the consequences.

This chapter delves into the details of these laws and principles.

Chapter 2

Laws of Magic

There are several ways that magic works. You have already discovered that your goal must first be created in the astral plane to manifest in the physical. Beyond that, you should layer the magic for additional power. To do so, make use of some well-established laws of magic. There is sympathetic magic, which has two laws: the Law of Similarity and the Law of Contagion. And there is religious magic, where the underlying law is reciprocity, or energy exchange, between devotee and deity.

Sympathetic Magic

Sympathetic magic is the overall heading for magical laws that utilize imitation, similarities, and correspondences in spell work. These can be broken down further into a law that relies on similarities, parallels, analogies, and the thought that "like produces like," and another law that relies on contagion, meaning that anything that was once in physical contact remains forever in magical contact. The following sections delve deeper into these two laws.

The Law of Similarity

The Law of Similarity is the concept that "like produces like." In New Age speak, a version of this is often called the Law of Attraction. The Law of Attraction version focuses on thoughts rather than spells, e.g., that positive thoughts bring positive results. The same is, of course, also valid in spell work.

The Law of Similarity is the reason that you should use correspondences when you develop spells. Symbols and items, drawings, and other correspondences are connected to the Law of Similarity because to create a goal on the astral plane, you use visualization.

We will look at symbols and correspondences in much greater depth in chapters 4 and 5.

Let's look at the Law of Similarity in action. For example, if you are trying to manifest wealth, you should use pentagrams and earth symbols, crystals, and coins or bills. These are all symbols of prosperity; they draw riches. If you are trying to manifest love in your life, you would use items associated with love, such as rose quartz, peridot, emerald, a heart-shaped item, a picture of Cupid, and maybe a red rose, because they draw love. In spells for transformation, the Law of Similarity is used to show that change is integral to the spell by including symbols that are known for transformation, such as a butterfly.

I also often include a drawing of what I am trying to manifest, as that is powerful Law of Similarity magic. When you focus on your intent while you draw what you want to manifest, you charge the picture with energy and emotion that further power your spell.

Another example of the Law of Similarity is the use of poppets. Poppets, or dolls that resemble a person, can be used to heal a person who has asked for healing, for example. The poppet is made to look like the person being healed in as many ways as possible, and the injury or illness is depicted in a way that can be removed. During the spell working, the spell worker removes the injury or illness from the poppet, with the intent to similarly remove the disease or damage from the person who is being healed. The Law of Similarity causes the ailment to be removed from the person because it was drawn out from the poppet.

Visualization is another key part of Similarity magic. When you visualize your goal while you do your spell, the Universe sees it the same way you do and adjusts accordingly. This is another way of stating that you must first create your goal in the astral plane to enable it to manifest in the physical.

The Law of Contagion

A powerful connection is held by things and persons who have been in physical contact. This is because what has been in physical contact remains forever in magical contact.

The Law of Contagion is why, when you have the permission to work magic for someone else, you should try to include some of their hair, a piece of their clothing, or any other item of theirs, as this directly connects the spell to that person. When you do candle magic, you can anoint the candle with bodily fluids (for example, saliva) from the person for whom you are doing the spell (with their permission, of course). Whenever you see mention of including something from the person that you are working a spell for, you see the Law of Contagion being utilized to connect the spell to the person the work is for.

Religious Magic

Religious magic, or divine magic, is practiced relatively similarly across most religions. You call on goddesses or gods for aid in accomplishing a goal (praying), and you give offerings to the deities in gratitude and as an energy exchange to get their attention. In Christianity, the offering may take the form of lighting a candle for a saint or giving alms to the poor. In polytheistic Witchcraft, it may mean placing out pieces of fish, bread, and garlic for Hekate, presenting Aphrodite with a fresh rose or a pearl necklace, or laying out a cup of mead and some pretty jewelry for Freya. (Later in this chapter, we will discuss appropriate offerings for a few deities from the Norse, Greek, and Hindu pantheons.)

In religious magic, a religious practitioner will work either with their patron deity or with the deity most aligned with their goal, and then they will call upon that god or goddess to manifest it. Ceremonial magicians and Kabbalists work with the Archangels. Some Pagans work with the Faeries.

When the practitioner prays to the deity, they may end the prayer with "So mote it be." *So mote it be* means "so be it," and it makes a statement an affirmation, even if it is phrased as a prayer. The word *amen* originally meant "so be it" in Judaism and Christianity. This is also how "amen" is usually translated in the Greek Old Testament.[2]

Remember that if you are asking for divine assistance in manifesting your goal, you must reciprocate. The offering to the deity with whom you are working is not optional. Fair energy exchange is needed, and not just between mortals! When a god or goddess feels that you are honoring them, they are much more likely to listen to and respond to your petition. Make sure that you have researched the deity so that you know what their likes and dislikes are. You would not want to offer a howling toy wolf to Njord, nor a squealing toy seagull to Skadi!

Gods and goddesses feel honored and respected when they know that you know them. If the deity you are working with has epithets, make sure that you know them and use the correct ones for the type of magic you are performing. Some gods have entirely different areas that they operate in, depending on the epithet.

When you call to the god or goddess, you need to ensure that they know that you are calling them specifically, not any other deity. Therefore, include their name, and if they have epithets, one or more of them. Also include different ways to describe the deity. Often two other forms are used, as three is a lucky number. Here is an example of how to call to Freya:

---

2. *Encyclopaedia Britannica*, s.v. "amen," last updated May 20, 2013, https://www .britannica.com/topic/amen-prayer.

꜀)))〗●●❲❲❲

I call upon thee, Freya, teacher of *seidr* and
owner of Brisingamen and Hildisvini.

꜀)))〗●●❲❲❲

If you intend to use religious magic, think about whether you always will be working with the same deity (maybe the Judeo-Christian God) or your patron deity, or whether each time you will work with a deity that is appropriate for the goal at hand. For example, if your goal is for your business to do well, you might want to work with Mercury. If your goal is to draw love, you might work with Aphrodite—careful there; she is not the faithful type. Maybe you want to choose Hymen, god of marriage, instead. If your goal is to increase your wisdom, you might want to work with Odin. If you want to do well in your studies, you might choose to work with Saraswati. Think it through. Decide how you will approach religious magic if you are going to work with it. Don't be afraid, however. No decision is cast in stone, and you can change approach at any time, as long as you honor the gods.

What to Offer to Some Well-Known Deities

As mentioned, if you are including religious magic in your work, you need to show the deity whose help you are requesting how much you appreciate them. An offering means that you give the deity the item. It is not a loan; it is a gift. You don't get it back after the spell has worked. You can include the item with the spell or build a small altar to the deity. If you later break down the altar, you can put items that decompose out in nature. Items that do not decompose should be kept in a special place for that deity. A box works.

In case you are unfamiliar with deities other than Abrahamic, I have included a few in this section. The gods that I have chosen to include are from pantheons that I have worked extensively with. Let me be clear that this list does not imply that these are the only deities that you can work with in religious magic. For example, I have not included the Christian God, Jesus, Mary, or any saint, as I do not have experience working with them in this fashion. You, of course, can work with them! Just do some research beforehand so that you make an appropriate offering.

Norse

The Norse pantheon consists of the Vanir gods, who are associated with fertility and abundance; the Æsir gods, who are associated with both war and order; and a few giants or half-giants, Jötunn, who were also considered part of the Æsir. The associations of the Vanir to fertility and the Æsir to war is weak, as the Æsir Thor is also associated with fertility and the Vanir fought mightily against the Æsir in a war between the divine tribes.

The Norse Gods that I have chosen to include are those I work with most often: the Vanir Frey, Freya, and their father Njord; the Æsir Odin, Thor, Heimdal, and Idun; and the Jötunn Skadi, who came to be included among the Æsir through marriage.

Freya

Freya is a goddess of beauty, love, fertility, war, and magic (*seidr*). Freya slept with dwarves in order to become the owner of the beautiful necklace Brisingamen. She likes jewelry, particularly gold jewelry. Amber is sacred to her, so any item with amber is a good offering. She also likes cats, as cats draw her chariot. She wears a cloak of falcon feathers, so pictures of such feathers or of falcons are appropriate offerings; this shows her that you have taken the time to get to know her. (Note that it is illegal to possess actual falcon feathers in the US.) Mead is always appreciated by her, and by any of the Norse gods. Apples are a good offering, too, as Idun's apples are what keep all of the Norse gods young(ish) and healthy.

Frey

Frey is a god of fertility. Therefore, wheat, oats, barley, or rye are appropriate offerings, as is bread. He is often depicted with a large penis, so phallic items are also suitable. Malt and malt-based beverages are also fitting.

Heimdal

Heimdal is a watchman and protects the Bifrost bridge. Offering Heimdal a bridge and a horn to blow shows him that you know him and that you honor his calling. He is also the one who instituted (as Rig) social order in the Norse world. You may disagree with the strict class structure that he introduced, but acknowledging his contribution will honor him. Living within the law and meeting social expectations is a great honor to Heimdal. Mead and pork are great offerings as well.

Idun

Idun has a tree with magical apples which keep the Norse gods young and healthy. Offering her apples or apple blossoms lets her know that you understand her role. She is also known to enjoy apple cider.

Njord

Njord is the Norse god of the sea. A small aquarium will please him, as will recorded sounds of seagulls or crashing waves. He enjoys fish dishes and seafood as well. He will greatly appreciate it if you bring an image or statue of him to the sea. You do not have to leave it there; he will appreciate the gesture, even if you take it back home with you.

Odin

Odin is a god of wisdom, poetry, death, runes, and many other things. Odin found the runes after hanging on a tree with nothing to eat or drink for nine days. Thus, he greatly appreciates offerings of food, mead, and water. Offering a set of runes is respectful. He also acquired the Mead of Poetry through shapeshifting and seduction. Offering poetry, especially if you have written it yourself, is highly appropriate. He has two ravens, Hugin and Munin, so he also appreciates pictures of ravens. He also has two wolves, Geri and Freki, which means anything associated with wolves is a good offering for him.

Skadi

Skadi is the Norse goddess of skiing and the snowy lands. She will enjoy a (miniature) set of skis or snowshoes. She will very much appreciate sprigs of pine, fir, or spruce, or incense made from the dried needles. A piece of the fur of an ermine, wolf, or another northern animal will also please her. She appreciates a good joke, so tell her one! Keep anything to do with bare feet away from here, lest you annoy her. (She had to choose her husband by looking only at the feet of the gods, and the pretty feet she chose turned out to belong to a god, Njord, with whom she was not at all compatible.)

Thor

Thor is the Norse god of thunder and lightning, high winds, and storms in general. Thor eats and drinks a LOT. Pork, mead, ale, bread—just about anything edible or drinkable is a good offering. Thor has two goats; when he slaughters them, he can restore them to life the following day, as long as the bones are intact. Therefore, offering him boneless goat meat is appropriate. Pictures of thunderbolts and storms are always a good choice.

Greek

The Greek pantheon is one of the most well known, and you may be familiar with these gods from reading texts like the *Iliad* and the *Odyssey*. Like the Norse gods, the Greek gods have human flaws. Be very certain to please the god before asking for their assistance.

The Greek gods each have many epithets, meaning words that describe their role and personality that are added to their name. One example is Hekate the Saffron-Clad. I am not listing epithets along with the god descriptions below. Researching the epithets of a god is an excellent way to understand who they are. Using an epithet that aligns with the magic you want to do is certain to please the god!

Apollo

Apollo is rational, logical, and orderly. He is a god of music as well as of the sun, and he carries a lyre. He can bring either good or ill health if he chooses to. He was born under a palm tree, so palms are sacred to him. A lyre or other string instrument is an appropriate offering, as are coconuts, pictures, or other depictions of the sun, as well as any object made of gold or that looks like gold.

Aphrodite

Aphrodite was born from a combination of the seafoam and the cut-off penis of her father, Uranus. When she was born, she was already an adult. She is often depicted on the shell of a scallop, and as such, shells are sacred to her. So are roses, pearls, doves, and swans. She will appreciate an offering of any of these items. She is a goddess of love and beauty, and any item associated with beauty or being attractive—e.g., a mirror, skincare, makeup, or perfume—will please her. She is also fond of chocolate and sweet wine such as port.

Ares

Ares is the god of war. He is impulsive and can be violent. He is a foot soldier rather than a strategically thinking high officer, unlike his sister Athena. He wears a helmet and carries a sword or a spear, and sometimes a shield. The same items that are good offerings for Athena are also good offerings for Ares, except for the owl.

Artemis

Artemis is the twin sister of Apollo. She is a goddess of the moon and the hunt, and she is a maiden, an unmarried woman. She carries a bow and arrow and is the protector of children, especially young girls. Her chariot is drawn by deer, which are sacred to her. In addition, she has several hunting dogs, gifts from Pan. Thus, a miniature bow and arrow, depictions of dogs, depictions of deer, and depictions of the moon are all excellent choices as offerings to Artemis.

Athena

Athena is a goddess of warfare strategy, artisanship, and wisdom. As a goddess of wisdom, owls are sacred to her. As a warfare goddess, spears and shields are as well. She is often shown as wearing a helmet. Any of these items constitute good offerings to Athena.

Demeter

Demeter is the goddess of grain, the harvest, and agriculture. Therefore, sheaves of wheat, baked goods, barley, fruits, and vegetables are all appropriate offerings. In addition, pigs are sacred to Demeter, so pork or any depiction of a pig are other good choices.

Dionysus

In many ways, Dionysus is the opposite of Apollo. Dionysus is the god of grapes, wine, vines, religious ecstasy, emotions, and chaos. He is often shown wearing leopard skin, so any depiction of a leopard is suitable as an offering. Likewise, all types of wine are appropriate, as are grape leaves and grapes.

Eros

Eros is a mischievous god of love and lust. He carries a bow and arrow and is depicted as a young man. All things sensual are good offerings for him: perfume, aphrodisiacs, erotic paintings, wine, fragrant massage oils, jewelry. A bow and arrow are, of course, appropriate.

Hekate

Hekate is known for appreciating simple things like leftovers. In ancient Greece, it was common to have a small box outside the door where offerings of bread, leftover fish, garlic, and other food items were left for Hekate. She is especially known to favor garlic. Dogs are her animals, so offering depictions of dogs works well. Among her symbols are keys and torches, and they will always please her. She is a liminal goddess, so she is an excellent choice to work with whenever you need to cross a boundary.

Hera

Hera is the wife of Zeus and the queen of heaven. She also likes to have her cup filled. As a queen, a crown is appropriate. Peacocks are sacred to Hera, so peacock feathers, peacock figurines, or any item with a peacock theme are fitting offerings. Hera is also the goddess of marriage, so any symbols of marital union—e.g., rings, handfasting cords, or a wedding cake—are suitable.

Hermes

Hermes is a messenger god and a psychopomp. He is the patron god of merchants and travelers, thieves, and those who need to be eloquent in their profession. He carries a caduceus and wears winged sandals and sometimes a winged hat or helmet. Because of his association with eloquence, any depiction of a tongue is a good offering, as are feathers, coins, or bills.

Hestia

Hestia is the goddess of the hearth. She is a fire goddess. Freshly baked homemade bread is a favorite offering of hers, as is a small fire. She also appreciates any depiction of a donkey, as she was once saved from danger by the braying of a donkey.

Iris

Iris is the goddess of the rainbow and the messenger for Hera. She is also the one who keeps the cups of the gods filled. Therefore, any depiction of a rainbow is suitable for Iris, as is a pitcher.

Persephone

Persephone started her life as Kore, the maiden goddess of flowers. As she grew through her teenage years, she looked for the meaning of her life; she wanted something more than making flowers. She was taken to the Underworld by Hades, where she became his bride and Persephone, Queen of the Underworld. She ate several pomegranate seeds that tied her to the Underworld while still allowing her to go to the surface each spring to reunite with her mother, Demeter. All flowers are sacred to Persephone and are good offerings. So are pomegranates, fancy crowns, and beautiful jewelry.

Poseidon

Poseidon is the god of the sea in the Greek Pantheon. He is also the god of earthquakes. He carries a trident and is regarded as the one who created horses. Ocean water makes a great offering for Poseidon, as does sea salt. Seaweed is also excellent. He always appreciates a trident.

Zeus

Zeus likes to have his cup full, so wine is a good offering. He is the king of the gods, so anything symbolizing royalty, such as a crown or scepter, is appropriate. All the Greek gods appreciate bay laurel. Dried bay leaf is fine. As Zeus is the god of thunder in the Greek pantheon, pictures of thunderbolts are an excellent offering.

Hindu

Hindu deities, as listed here, are still worshipped today in India. When working with gods of a living religion, there is always a risk of cultural appropriation or being accused of cultural appropriation. While living in India, it has been my experience that Hindus are delighted when they find that a Westerner honors their Gods. After first checking for appropriateness with family and friends, I have held Wiccan rituals working with Hindu gods and with Hindu participants. I have had nothing but positive reactions. If you are earnest in your study and truly honor the gods, you are on solid ground.

The Hindu gods appreciate being dressed in beautiful garments, getting garlands of flowers, having incense and candles lit near them or in front of them, and being given ghee, coconut, and fruits. All appreciate having the feet of their statue washed with devotion as an honoring.

If you plan to work with a Hindu deity, please first give an offering to Lord Ganesh. Ganesh is the lord of all new beginnings and the remover of obstacles. He is worshipped before any other deity to remove anything that could hinder the successful worship of the god.

Brahma

Brahma is the creator god, now largely in the background. Water pots, bowls to receive alms, the Vedas, rosaries, spoons or ladles to pour libations or liquid sacrifices with, and lotuses are sacred to him and make excellent offerings. His vehicle (the object he rides) is a swan.

Durga

Durga is a form of Parvati. Durga is a warrior and a demon-slayer who rides on a tiger or a lion. In India, goats and buffalos are sacrificed to her. Ghee, coconut, sesame seeds, fruit (especially bananas), sugar, sweets (any sweet will be much appreciated, though she is known to especially favor those that are white in color), milk, and honey are all traditional offerings to Durga.

Kali

Kali is a form of Durga and thus a form of Parvati. She is a destroyer of ignorance and evil and is prone to ecstatic dancing. She is a fearsome-looking goddess with a garland of human heads around her neck and a skirt of human arms. Her tongue often sticks out, and her eyes are bloodshot. However, in the Northeast of India, especially, she is seen as a protective and even nurturing mother goddess, Kali-Ma. Kali is the goddess to work with if your ego is getting in the way of your success. Kali appreciates hibiscus flowers, has a sweet tooth, and likes cooked rice, cooked lentils, and yogurt.

Kamadeva

Kamadeva is the Hindu god of love and lust. Like his Greek counterpart Eros, he carries a bow and arrow. His symbols are bees, a parrot, and a cuckoo bird. Mango and a paste of sandalwood are some favorites of his. The paste is available ready-made as a beauty product.

Lakshmi

Lakshmi is the goddess of good fortune, prosperity, and beauty. Lakshmi is drawn to clean houses to bestow prosperity on the inhabitants. She favors perfume, items made of sandalwood, and items with saffron. (Note: sustainably grown sandalwood can be purchased from Australia.) She is fond of gold and the color pink.

Parvati

Parvati is the wife of Shiva. She is the goddess of stable marriage and family. She is fond of flowers, especially red ones, and she also is attracted to red bangles and red cloth.

Saraswati

Saraswati is the goddess of wisdom, learning, knowledge, and the arts, especially music. Peacocks, swans, and lotus flowers are sacred to her and make good offerings, as do books, pen and paper, musical instruments, and painting supplies. She also appreciates yellow flowers and anything with saffron.

Shiva

Shiva is the destroyer and the recreator. If you have beliefs that limit your ability to succeed and you need to destroy these beliefs, working with Shiva is perfect. He is usually shown with a cobra, a *trishula* (trident), and the first sliver of the new moon. He is said to enjoy sweets made from milk, as well as a mixture of yogurt, milk, sugar, ghee, and honey. He also favors saffron mixed with milk.

Vishnu

Vishnu is the preserver. He carries a conch shell, a discus (wheel), a lotus flower, and a mace. A mace is a kind of club made of metal. Vishnu saves the world when it is in danger by descending to earth as a mortal avatar. He has come as a fish, a turtle or a tortoise, a boar, a lion man, a dwarf, four men, and a yet-to-come fifth man. All of these are symbols of his and make good offerings. His Krishna avatar was very fond of ghee, butter, and milk, so these make excellent offerings.

Spell for Prosperity Using Religious Magic

Lakshmi is a goddess who brings prosperity to those who keep their house clean. In this spell, there is an offering to her in the form of cleaning up a mess in the home to please her, and then there is a request for her to bestow prosperity.

In this example of religious magic,

You will need

A photo or drawing of a messy part of your home: dirty dishes, an unmade bed, or similar

A picture or statue of Kamadhenu, the Hindu "cow of plenty," or another cow

A photograph or drawing of the messy part of your home after you have cleaned it up (done the dishes, made the bed, etc.) with the picture or statue of Kamadhenu or cow visible in the clean space

A statue, picture, drawing, or other representation of the goddess Lakshmi

A brazier or other way of burning one of the pictures

Cloth to present to the representation of Lakshmi

A table or horizontal surface to work on

High-percentage isopropyl alcohol

Epsom salt

Long matches

To prepare yourself and your space,

YOU WILL NEED

Oils, herbs, or scented candles that connect you with deity and that support prosperity. Cinnamon, basil, and cloves are suggested

If possible, garments for yourself that are pink and gold, or garments with gold accents

Sweet-smelling incense, e.g., fruit or rose

If available, a lotus-shaped candle holder

A clean cloth for your table surface

Take a picture of a mess in your house. If your home has no messes (impressive!), take a picture of dirty dishes before you wash them. Clean up the mess, then place a picture or statue of Kamadhenu (goddess cow of plenty, here representing prosperity) or any depiction of a cow in the now-cleaned-up space. Then take a picture of the clean area with the cow in it. Print out both the image of the mess and the image of the cleaned-up space.

Clean the space where you will be working the spell. Make sure it is decluttered.

Take a preparatory bath before you proceed. Cinnamon, basil, and cloves are appropriate oils and fragrances for this working, as cinnamon helps you connect with deity, and basil and cloves both support prosperity. If you only have a shower, you can instead use scented candles while you shower.

If possible, dress in pink with white and gold accents to perform the spell. Lakshmi is often depicted wearing pink, so this is a color known to be pleasing to her.

To prepare your space for casting the spell, burn a sweet-smelling incense, such as a rose- or fruit-scented one, or have a scented candle lit. If you have a lotus-shaped candle holder, use that. Lotus flowers are sacred to Lakshmi and will please her. A scented spray will also work. You want your home to smell pleasant and inviting.

On the surface where you will work, place a clean cloth and a statue of Lakshmi; a silver figure is ideal. Dress the statue in a beautiful clean cloth wrapped like a sari. If a statue is not feasible, use a picture of Lakshmi pouring out gold coins. Lean that picture on a supporting object on the work surface so that the picture stands up and does not fall.

Next, place the picture of the cleaned-up space faceup on the work surface in front of Lakshmi, and place the picture of the mess facedown. You don't want Lakshmi to be looking at the mess. She should see only the cleaned-up space.

Light a small fire in a brazier. Use high-percentage isopropyl alcohol poured over Epsom salt, and light it with long (fireplace) matches so that you don't risk burning your fingers. (See chapter 10 for how to create a fire this way.)

Crumple up the photo that has the mess on it and state:

))))))●●●((((

Lakshmi, goddess of prosperity and wealth, thou who is also called Sri, goddess of beauty, lady with the lotus and the elephants and the gold, come to me! I honor thee; I worship thee; I ask thee to share thy wealth with me.

Lakshmi, my home is clean. In thy honor, to please thee and pay homage to thee, I burn all that is disorderly, messy, and unclean.

(Now, burn the picture of the mess using the fire in the brazier.)

In thy honor, in adoring reverence of thee, I have cleaned my home and scented it with sweet fragrances for thee to take pleasure in.

Thou goddess of abundance and plenty, I ask a boon of thee, that thou may share thy wealth with me, so that I may have all that I need, and more to spare, and more to share.

)))))●●●((((

Now pick up the picture of the cow in the clean, neat space and hold it in front of you. Envision the goddess Lakshmi in front of you. Visualize how she places her hands in blessing of you and sends her divine energy to the crown of your head.

Draw in that divine energy through the top of your head. Send it to your heart, then out through your projective arm, through the photo or drawing, through the cow in the photo or drawing, and up through your receptive arm, while focusing on prosperity of all forms. If you are right-handed, the right arm is your projective arm, and the left is your receptive arm. If you are left-handed, your left arm is projective and the right is receptive.

If you are seated, stand up now. Wave and flap your picture joyously as you chant:

)))ﾩﾮﾭﾫ(((

Home is straightened, home is cleaned
And myself I also preened
Lakshmi comes to where I dwell
And I prosper from this spell
All I need does come to me
As I will, so mote it be!

)))ﾩﾮﾭﾫ(((

Shout, "Yes, Lakshmi, you hear me! For the greatest good of all, so mote it be." Now purposefully release the energy you have raised, i.e., send your spell out to the Universe.

Then sit down and take a few deep breaths. And remember to keep your abode clean!

Supper for Prosperity Using Religious Magic

You will need

A table that can be set for a meal

An as-elegant-as-possible table setting for deity

Foods that are known to be favored by the god or goddess you
    have chosen to work with

A table setting and a meal for yourself, if you wish

Set a table setting for a prosperity deity. Make it as elegant and inviting as possible, with delicacies known to be favored by the god or goddess you've chosen.

Speak out loud, inviting the deity. Be certain to call them by name and with at least two attributes so that the god knows that only they are being addressed. Offer them the meal and ask for their assistance in achieving prosperity. Then take your leave, or sit with them for some time, eating your own meal. You will know that the god has arrived by feeling their presence, not in the physical sense, but in the spiritual and emotional. You may feel elated; calm, peaceful, and free of anxiety; or immensely loved. You may feel awe and wonder. You may feel an inner strength that you never before knew that you had.

Let the meal for the deity sit out for the night. In the morning, thank the god for their presence and place the food out where animals will eat it.

Combining the Laws of Magic

Many who work magic will layer their religious magic with the Law of Similarity and the Law of Contagion. Thus, they will use correspondences, drawings, visualizations, and other means to layer a religiously based spell. In addition, the practitioner may also add physical items that have been in contact with themselves or the person for whom they are creating the spell.

When you set a goal, look for similarities that you can employ. If you are working on a spell to help you feel grounded and stable, you could use a picture of a pole cemented into the ground. A photo, drawing, or a description of a meditating Buddhist monk, a praying Christian monk, or a meditating Hindu yogi would also be a good similarity.

Think about what items you could use to apply the Law of Contagion to a goal of yours. Since the goal is for you, some strands of your hair would be perfect. A word of caution: hair smells bad if you burn it!

Chapter 2

Ethics of Magic

Actions have consequences. That applies to spells and magic as well.

First and foremost, it is unethical to influence the free will of someone else. It is, with few exceptions, unethical to cast a spell regarding someone else without their consent.

Only use what you learn in this book for benevolent purposes. Then you are performing welfare magic, and only good will come to you. *Welfare magic* is magic for your personal spiritual development or that of others, or for manifesting positives in your life or that of others. This does include prosperity!

If you use this knowledge for nefarious purposes, you are performing *misfortune magic*, and you probably won't like the results. Misfortune magic is exactly what it sounds like: magic to cause adversity of any kind, including illness or death, in the life of someone else.

In the end, it all comes back to one word: karma! If you interfere with the lives of others, you probably won't like the consequences when karma interferes with your own life. I use the word *karma* here in the way it is often used in the West, meaning the effects will take place in this lifetime.

Many spell workers believe in the Threefold Law: what you send out comes back to you threefold. Usually, this means that it will come back to you on three different levels. Send out positive, receive positive on three levels. Send out negative, receive negative on three levels.

Typically, you first receive energy back on the physical level, then on the mental level, and finally on the spiritual level. The return on the physical level involves your body, health, or belongings. The return on the level of the mind affects your reputation, mental health, or amount of success in a current undertaking. The return on the spiritual level acts on your spiritual welfare. It affects your connection with the Divine, whether you fear death or understand the purpose of your life, or how active you are in your personal religious practice, if you have one.

That said, every ethic is a situational ethic: you may opt to protect yourself and your kin because, in the end, the karmic balance may be in your favor if you do so. For example, if someone is prowling your neighborhood and stealing pets and valuables, and they have somehow managed to penetrate the shields and wards you had set up, it is perfectly ethical to cast a spell for the person to be caught by the police.

The best rule to follow is "harm none." Even "harm none" is a situational ethic. If, with magic or otherwise, you could save an entire continent from famine and disease forever, but one single person will die somewhere on a different continent because of your work, would you do it? Janet Farrar used this example in a workshop I took from her and Gavin Bone several years ago. Think about it.

Examples of Ethical Spells

It is always ethical for you to do spell work for your own small child. Just as you have the right to make medical and other decisions for them, you can do spell work for them. When the child is old enough to understand whether they want the outcome or not, you need their consent, just as with anyone else.

It is always ethical for you to do spell work for your pets and livestock. In this section, I'll be sharing other examples of ethical spell work.

A Spell to Draw Love to You

A spell to draw love to you does not interfere with the will of anyone in particular. It enhances your lovability and perceived lovability, and it increases the probability that someone you meet will fall in love with you. (In chapter 9, we'll talk about making a honey jar for precisely this purpose.)

A Spell to Be Better at Cross-Generational Relationships

Again, this does not interfere with the will of anyone in particular. It enhances your ability to communicate across generational gaps and increases the probability that you will get along with people of other generations.

Sending Healing Energy to Someone Who Requested It

If someone has requested healing, by all means, do a healing spell for them. They have requested it, they want it, and your spell will improve their chances of getting well. Go for it! Remember that your magic should always be in addition to medical care, never instead of it. Magic instead of medical care would be unethical, harmful, and potentially illegal.

Any Spell for a Person Who Requested It, Within Reason

As long as the requested spell does not interfere with the will of any particular person, doing a spell for others who have requested it is ethical. Some words of caution: it is much safer to do magic for people you know and whose situation you understand. A random stranger may ask you to do a spell for them that they think is best for them in their current situation, but you might have chosen to do something different had you understood their situation better.

Imagine that a person comes to you and asks you to perform a spell that will draw someone wealthy to them to be their spouse.

If you knew the person, you would know that they had lost their job some time ago, and they are desperate to get their finances in order. You would also know that this person had always had a well-paying position and earned their own money. You might discuss with them whether a spell for a new job would be a better solution. But if you did not know the person, you may not be able to have that conversation. In that case, you might go ahead and do the spell to draw someone wealthy to them to be their spouse, only for the person to end up married to an affluent spouse, but incredibly bored and unhappy without a fulfilling job.

Examples of Unethical Spells

Any spell that interferes with the free will of someone is unethical. The following are examples of unethical spells.

A Spell to Make Someone Like You Better or Heal the Rift Between You

If you have a difficult relationship with a family member, for example, you might think of casting a spell to make them think more highly of you. Don't. That would be a perfect example of interfering with the free will of another person. This kind of spell work is unethical; leave it be. Instead, work on repairing the relationship face-to-face.

Sending Healing Energy to Someone Who Did Not Request It

Sending healing to someone who did not request it brings us to an example I was taught when I was a witchling in training. It was the story of two people, Aunt Milda and Uncle Hyland.

Aunt Milda is in the hospital. She is married to Uncle Hyland, and unbeknownst to you, Uncle Hyland has been emotionally abusing Aunt Milda lately. Aunt Milda wants to stay in the marriage for her own reasons, but she is exhausted. A few days in the hospital gives her a respite and a chance to recoup her energy. She does not want to speed up her physical healing and be discharged by her physician earlier than necessary—she really does not. Do not send Aunt Milda healing unless she has asked for it!

Clarity of Intent

When writing a spell, clarity of intent is of the utmost importance. A typical example of spell work gone wrong is the person who did a spell asking for $750 and then received a $750 reimbursement check for medical bills they previously had paid. The spell worked, but not the way they intended it to work. Even worse, what if the check was the inheritance from your favorite relative, who passed away right after you did your spell? That is *not* what you had hoped would happen. There are lots and lots and lots of variations on the concept of a spell gone wrong, and they all share one characteristic: the spells are overly general. Being specific is a much safer path.

Therefore, if you are a carpet salesperson, for example, your spell should be something like, "I make $1,000 in profits in the next week from selling carpets. For the greatest good of all, so mote it be." When doing spell work regarding money, find a way to earn money that is appropriate for you. Doing an "I win the lottery" spell is rarely effective. There are so many people putting that spell out into the Universe in various ways that the Universe cannot possibly make them all true at once. Remember, magic is not miracles. Magic is making the possible probable. So, an "I win the lottery" spell *will* increase your chances of winning. It just will not guarantee it, and it can only move the needle so much for you.

Positive and Present

Always write a spell in the positive and in the present tense.

"I will not eat bananas anymore starting tomorrow" is not a suitable spell formulation. First, tomorrow never comes. It is always and forever today. When you wake up tomorrow, it is still your today. A spell affecting tomorrow, therefore, will always have its effect in the future. It will not change anything today, so it will never come into effect. Therefore, tweak number one would be to rewrite the spell as "I do not eat bananas." However, that is still not a great spell because the Universe is not good at understanding the words *not*, *no*, or *never*.

Please, do not think of a banana wearing a red baseball cap and skiing in a slalom race.

If you immediately envisioned a banana skiing in a slalom race while wearing a red baseball cap, you are just like the Universe.

Therefore, the next tweak is to rewrite the spell as "I eliminate bananas from my diet." That is better, but it still mentions bananas. The spell's focus is still on the wrong thing. Tweak the spell to include a list of fruits that you would like to eat instead: "The fruits I eat are primarily apples, oranges, mangos, guavas, and pears."

Exercise: Affirmations

You WILL NEED

Pen and paper

A place to work undisturbed

Practice what you have learned by writing an affirmation about what you want your life to be like. Write it in the positive and in the present. It is a goal, and spell-work is about manifesting a goal of some sort. Here are some examples:

- I have a home, food on the table, and reliable transportation. I am employed with a wage or salary that meets my needs and have enough money to spare for my wants.

- I have good close friends. My sex life is great. I find joy in life.

- I set appropriate boundaries.

- I love myself, and I am worthy of love.

Write the affirmation down on a piece of paper and say it out loud every single morning. If time in the morning is tight, have the paper laminated and hang it in the shower. Every time you say your affirmation, visualize it as being already real and manifest.

Creating Your Goal

Affirmations are the beginning of spell work. When you write a spell, you state the goal that you want to manifest in the form of an affirmation, and then you layer the magic using the Law of Similarity, the Law of Contagion, and other methods we will talk more about later. Many practitioners use the word *intent* or *intention* when referring to the goal of a spell.

In project management or elsewhere, you may have come across the concept of SMART goals. This concept is equally important in spell work. Choose SMART goals that you intend to magically support the manifestation of.

- We have already covered what the S stands for: Specific.

- M is for measurable. You need to have a way to know when you have manifested your goal. The earlier example of $1,000 in carpet sales is a good one; this goal is measurable.

- A is for Aligned, or, in some variations, Attainable or Achievable. The following section addresses that aspect as you examine whether your ecosystem is aligned with your goal.

- R is for Reasonable, Relevant, or Realistic. The goal has to be possible, and reasonably so, for the spell to make it probable.

- T is for timely. It must be possible for the goal to manifest before it is irrelevant. We'll discuss this a bit later in the chapter.

Exercise: Create Goals

YOU WILL NEED

Pen and paper

A place to work undisturbed

Look at your list of affirmations from the previous exercise. Is each in the positive and the present? Is each affirmation Specific, Measurable, Reasonable, Relevant, and Realistic? (You will deal with Aligned and Timely in a later exercise.)

Take your affirmations and turn them into SM(A)R(T) goals. You will work with these goals in the following exercises if they pass the test of the next section.

If you need to add additional goals, here are some ideas to get you going:

- What do you need to feel safe and secure?

- What kind of place do you want to live in?

- What kind of prosperity do you want?
- What brings you joy in life?
- What do you need to be physically and emotionally satisfied?
- What boundaries do you want to set?
- What level of ambition do you strive for?
- What do you need to love yourself?
- How do you wish to communicate?
- What do you want to learn and understand?
- How do you want your spiritual life to be?

Ensuring a Successful Spell

Now that you have a list of goals, it is time to ask yourself some questions. You need to be fully invested in manifesting a particular goal for your spell to succeed. You need to think through whether you have what it takes to reach your goal or whether you need to acquire new resources, skills, or knowledge. You need to understand any harmful consequences that might result from the goal being manifest. You can start answering these questions by performing the following exercise.

Exercise: Check the Ecosystem

Now it is time to ascertain that your goals are Aligned.

You will need

The list of goals that you created in the previous exercise

Pen and paper

A place to work undisturbed

For each of your goals, ask yourself the following questions. Think carefully before answering them, and be honest with your answers. This part of the preparation for spell work may take days or weeks.

- If the goal I have in mind were to manifest, would there be any negative consequences? Any at all? Is there a way to mitigate any negative consequences? If not, do I really want to proceed?

- Are my family and friends and other support systems in favor of this goal manifesting? If not, how do I change that? If they are not in favor, why are they not in favor? How does manifesting this goal affect them? Do they believe it is possible, or do they think it is futile? What would it take for them to buy into my goal? Am I willing to go ahead with this goal, even if it may rob me of my current support system? Is there another support system on which I can rely?

- Is there anything at my home, job, school, etc., that I need to change to manifest this goal? If so, how will I do that? Am I willing to do that? Are there any adverse consequences of making those changes? If so, can I mitigate those negative consequences?

- What resources are needed to manifest this goal? Do I have them? If not, how will I acquire them?

- Do I have to give up anything to manifest this goal? Am I willing to do that?

- Is my behavior consistent with manifesting this goal? Do I need to change anything about how I act for this goal to manifest? If so, how will I go about that? What do I need to do?

- What skills are needed to manifest this goal? Do I need additional skills for this goal to manifest? If so, how will I acquire them? Are these other skills related to any changes in behavior that are needed?

- Why do I want to manifest this goal? Is there real value for me in manifesting this goal? Why do I think that there is value in manifesting this goal? Do I believe that manifesting this goal is for the greatest good of all? Am I motivated to manifest this goal? Do I firmly believe that I can take the steps needed to manifest this goal? If not, what do I need to do to become confident that I can?

- What is my reason for existing in this lifetime? Does manifesting this goal fit in with my reason for existence? Is manifesting this goal consistent with my spirituality? Will it make me more closely connected to deity? Does it need to do so?

If you find that any of your goals need tweaking or need to be replaced after answering the screening questions, be certain to do so. You need to have a good, solidly documented intention to proceed with building a spell.

You may want to mark this exercise so you can come back to these questions in the future. Before working any spell for a specific purpose, you should always ask yourself these same questions.

Using Divination

The final step in ensuring that it is wise to proceed with a spell is often to perform a divination. It can be as straightforward as a one-card tarot draw, asking the question "What will be the outcome of performing this spell?" or "Should I cast this spell?" Heed the answer. If you get the Three of Swords, you need to rethink what you are planning. Or, instead of pulling a tarot card, you could draw a rune or use another divination system you are familiar with.

If you do not use any divination system, either ask a friend to do a reading for you or meditate on the appropriateness of your goal and abide by what comes to you. For a meditation, you can refer back to the ecosystem questions and think about your answers one by one. Close your eyes, breathe deeply, and search your innermost feelings about the answer that you gave.

If you are working with a deity, you can ask the god whether you should cast the spell and then listen for a response.

Point in Time Placement

Finding when your goal should manifest is an integral part of the process. First, investigate how you see time. I mean that literally. Think about when you got out of bed this morning. Where, in time, did that happen? Is it behind you? Is it straight to your left? In front of you to your left? In front of you to the right? Is it under you? Above you? Some other place?

Go back further, say to your most recent birthday. Where in time is it located?

Go back to an event in high school, maybe the prom or graduation or another momentous occasion. Where is it located?

Now, think of something that is yet to happen. When will you next brush your teeth? Where is that found in time? What about your next birthday?

Then, establish where *right now* is on the timeline.

Now, what you have accomplished is establishing your personal timeline—your view of time. For some people, time is a straight line. For some people, it curves. For some people, it is a spiral. It doesn't matter what the shape is as long as you know where the past is, where the present is, and where the future is.

Exercise: Timeline

YOU WILL NEED

Your list of goals

An area free of obstacles so that you can walk at least ten feet in any direction from where you are standing

Pick one of the goals you established. Visualize the timeline you've established on the floor in front of you. Go to the place on the timeline that is your "now" by physically walking your body to that point on the envisioned timeline, then turn your body toward the direction you found to be the future.

Now picture your goal already manifest in the physical plane, with all the colors, sounds, smells, tastes, and feelings that are attached to that goal when manifest. Bring your goal along and stroll in the direction of the future. You will sense where you should place your goal on the timeline. It may be a different point than you first expected. Visualize your goal as manifest on this point on the timeline and stand there for a moment; you can face either the future or the present for this part. Enjoy the victory of your goal being manifest. See what you will see, hear what you will hear, smell what you will smell, and feel what you will feel when your goal has come true. Live the moment! Feel the joy!

With your goal placed at its proper place on the timeline, create a link to it. The link might be a visualization of a silvery thread or anything that keeps you permanently connected to the goal. Then look toward the present. Look at what just preceded the goal being manifest. Ask yourself, *What was the last step?* Then take a step toward the present on your timeline and ask yourself, *What was the action just before that final step?*

Leave your goal where it belongs on the timeline, and slowly start walking the timeline back toward the present. Make sure that your connection to the goal stays solid as you walk back. Take careful note of all the steps you had taken, everything you did along the way, to manifest your goal. When you get back to the present, write down all the steps that you saw. You will use this technique as part of a spell in chapter 14.

Take a deep breath and look again at where the goal is on your timeline. Is the goal still relevant at that point? If not, rethink.

Chapter 3

)))))●●●●(((((

MAGICAL TIMING

Knowing when to cast a spell is vital for its success. The better the stars are aligned to support your goal, the better the magic is layered, and the more conditions are in your favor. This chapter will teach you how to use the sun, the moon, and the planets to determine when the best time to cast your spell is, and how to use their power to enhance your spell work.

Lunar Timing

The scientific community and the magical community use slightly different names for the phases of the moon. Knowing both sets of terms will help you when you read about the moon.

Moon Shape	Magical Name (Common)	Astronomical Name
●	Dark Moon	New Moon
☽	New Moon	Waxing Crescent
◑	First Quarter	First Quarter
◐	Gibbous	Waxing Gibbous
○	Full Moon	Full Moon
○	Disseminating	Waning Gibbous
◐	Last Quarter	Last Quarter or Third Quarter
☾	Balsamic	Waning Crescent

The dark moon rises at about the same time and place as the sun and sets about the same time and place as the sun. Yes, every time. The moon then rises and sets later and later until, at the time of the full moon, she rises in the evening and sets in the morning!

As a rough statement, the moon rises in the east and sets in the west. Depending on where you are located and the time of year, this may not take place at exactly due east and due west. The best way to make sure that you can see the moon setting is to face west, with a clear view to the west, southwest, and northwest.

Moon Phase	Moonrise	Moonset
Dark Moon	Sunrise	Sunset
First Quarter	Noon	Midnight

Moon Phase	Moonrise	Moonset
Full Moon	Sunset	Sunrise
Third Quarter	Midnight	Noon

As you might already have guessed, it is recommended to do different types of magic during different phases of the moon. Because the energy is different in each phase, what you can accomplish is different as well. The following sections will explain the lunar phases and the types of magic they correspond with.

Dark Moon

The dark moon is dark and silent, quietly anticipating the new moon. If you feel like you need to step back for a moment and practice introspection, the dark moon is the perfect time for a temporary withdrawal. If you need to formulate new goals, choose the dark moon as the time to do so. This is also a good time to make plans for Acting in Accord. If you are about to take action, wait! Do not take action during the dark moon, when emotions may run high. Instead, ask yourself the "Check the Ecosystem" questions from chapter 2.

This is the time to do magic that aims to clarify your intents and goals, and magic that blesses your dreams and goals. One way of doing so is to perform divination to determine what magic you need to work. If you feel that you are experiencing a lack of clarity, do not worry. This is normal—some things are hidden from you during the dark moon. Meditate to find whatever clarity is available to you now, then wait until later in the moon cycle to learn more.

If you did not do retrospective work during the balsamic moon preceding the dark moon, the dark moon is also an excellent time to do this.

New Moon

The new moon is just a sliver of light in the sky. It brings a sense of excitement and anticipation of something new and fresh to come. The new moon is the time to manifest! The moon has gone from nothing to something; that is what you want for manifestations. All of the growing phases work for manifestation, but this phase— Diana's Bow, the Bow of Artemis—is the strongest.

The new moon is a time to commit to your goals. Get ready to get going! If you have a nascent project, this is the time to do magic for it to take solid form and for the plans to become a reality. If you have made plans for Acting in Accord and need to gather resources to execute your strategy, do your resource gathering during the new moon. Get excited about what you are about to embark on! Do magic to manifest the resources needed for your purposes.

Go out and curtsy or bow to the new moon. State three goals. Doing so is time-honored and straightforward magic.

First Quarter

The moon is halfway to full. The first quarter is a good phase in which to take action and start executing your Acting in Accord plan.

The first quarter is an excellent time to work with deities that support new undertakings. One good choice is Ganesh, the Remover of Obstacles and Lord of All Beginning. Do magic to remove obstacles that will hinder you from manifesting your goal. Also, do magic to bless new beginnings. If you have a project that has started but needs a push, first quarter is the time to do magic for it to flourish.

Gibbous Moon (Waxing Gibbous)

The moon is nearly full. If you have a project that seems to have plateaued—a project that is almost successful but has run into some last-minute challenges—this is the time to do magic for it to become unstuck and grow into its full potential. This is the time to do magic for projects to complete successfully.

If you are working on Acting in Accord for a goal and wonder if your plan is working, assess your situation under a gibbous moon. If your plan is not working, this is a good time to revise it. Do magic to support any changes in your plans.

Full Moon

The moon is in its fullest glory. If you have a project that has succeeded, this is the time to celebrate and thank the moon. You are not thinking about the wrap-up yet, only that you have accomplished what you set out to do.

The full moon is shining with Her full might on you. Everything is lit; there is nothing in the shadow. That means that now you can gain full clarity, as there is nothing hidden any longer. If you are wondering whether the goal you are working on needs to be tweaked, do so under a full moon. Ask yourself all the "Check the Ecosystem" questions again. Also, ensure that you are checking on your Acting in Accord plan. The full moon is another good time to assess the plan and verify that you have all the resources that you need. When everything is in order, put ALL your energy into the plan under a full moon. This is a time for nonstop action, movement, dancing, and joy!

Do divination by looking at the full moon in a scrying mirror or a bowl of still water, with or without oil on the surface.

Disseminating Moon (Waning Gibbous)

The moon has started to shrink. The disseminating moon is a time for banishings, though major banishings can wait until just before the dark moon. Also, listen to the word *disseminating*; to disseminate means to spread widely. Consider whether you have anything that you can or need to share with others.

If you learned something from what you have done recently, this is the time to document your new knowledge. If you are planning to give back to the community or if you are thinking of doing volunteer work, use the disseminating moon to schedule the start of your undertaking. If you plan to give a lecture, be on a radio or TV show, or lead a workshop, the disseminating moon is the time to do so.

Last Quarter

The moon is halfway gone. Now is the best time to perform the retrospective assessment of how your recent work went.

When your Acting in Accord work is nearing completion, plan to start the wrap-up under a last-quarter moon. Make sure that you know what you still have left to do in order to succeed and that you document all learnings. If there are things that could have gone better, you need to take this opportunity to learn so you can have an improved outcome in the future. The last quarter is an excellent time to do magic to analyze completed plans and successfully maximize your learning.

Balsamic Moon

The moon is nearly gone. There is only a sliver of light left in the sky. The word *balsamic* means healing or restorative; curative. The balsamic moon is the time to do major, significant banishing or healing spells. This is when the moon is about to go from something to nothing, which is precisely what you want when you need something to go away.

The balsamic moon is an excellent time to do magic for letting go of emotional ties that no longer serve you, bad habits, and anything that needs to leave your life. If you suffer from any type of addiction, the time to address it with magic is under the balsamic moon, and the balsamic moon is also the time to enter a recovery program. This is the time to do spells that help you let go, as well as spell work to heal from old wounds. This is also a good time to do healing magic in general; draw on the healing and curative properties of this phase.

Astrological Timing

Astrological timing is based on the stars and planets observed in the sky. If you are brand new to astrology, I recommend Kevin Burk's *Astrology: Understanding the Birth Chart.* The website www.astro .com is an excellent source to learn from, as is cafeastrology.com. All of the above start with the natal chart, which is based on where and when someone was born. Astrological information about signs and houses is also applicable when determining whether a given time is suitable for doing a particular kind of magic, which is our aim here.

To understand astrological timing, first look at where the sun is. The sun cycles through the twelve zodiac signs once a year, so it is not always practical to wait to do magic until the sun is in the sign that most strongly supports your spell. If you can find support for a goal that you are working on in the zodiac sign that the sun is currently in, be sure to include this in your working. You can add it in by mention or by drawing the sun and the zodiac sign symbol.

You should also look at where the moon and the planets are before doing magic, as they have correspondences as well. Purchase an astrological calendar or look up a free astrological chart online. You can also get this information via smartphone apps. Astrological calendars will tell you what sign and house (or section of the sky) the sun is in for a time, as well as what astrological sign the moon and the other planets are currently in.

The following chart shares some planetary correspondences.

Planetary Body	Symbol	Characteristics: What the Planet Does
Sun	☉	Gives purpose and power. Defines our most obvious purpose in life. Seizes the moment. Keeps focus on the present, the here and now. Shows itself to the world. Bolsters the ego, sometimes to a fault. Represents the outer self: what is visible.
Moon	☽	Gives intuition and psychic abilities. Represents the inner self: what is hidden. Nourishes. Opens to the astral realm. Intuits. Remembers. Can cause weepiness and overwrought emotional reactions.
Mercury	☿	Communicates. Articulates. Thinks. Creates ideas. Categorizes and sorts. Focuses on details; sometimes misses the big picture.
Venus	♀	Manifests resources. Creates beauty. Relates and loves. Creates harmony.

Planetary Body	Symbol	Characteristics: What the Planet Does
Mars	♂	Takes action. Manages anger (or not!). Asserts and, if limited, fights. Awakens the warrior. Personifies ambition. Gives drive and energy. Focuses. Does—is all about doing.
Jupiter	♃	Expands! Causes expansion. Sees possibilities. Personifies abundance. Manifests possibilities into reality. Brings good fortune. Trusts and hopes. Triggers generosity. Reminds you to be grateful. Manages risk. Philosophizes and handles religious beliefs, morals, and social values. Stresses honor in all actions. Creates fun, optimism, and success. Causes over-optimism by offering rose-colored glasses.
Saturn	♄	Creates rules and regulations. Narrows the focus onto responsibility. Puts structure in place. Creates boundaries. Limits. Enhances self-discipline. Is stern. Represents authority. Teaches lessons. Triumphs over obstacles. Supports lasting achievements. Can cause fear.

Planetary Body	Symbol	Characteristics: What the Planet Does
Uranus	♅	Causes change, as it is ever the change agent. Creates and supports inventions. Supports rebellion. Thinks outside-of-the-box. Is unpredictable and causes instability in systems. Represents science and genius. Is eccentric and does the unexpected. Can be revolutionary.
Neptune	♆	Gives inspiration. Brings spirituality and can put people into dreamtime. Bolsters magic. Strengthens intuition. Moves forward through evolution rather than revolution. Fools through deception. Beguiles and deceives through illusion.
Pluto	♇	Causes transformation. Forces the cycle of death and rebirth. Causes destruction. Encourages, but also removes, vices. Enables letting go. Draws prosperity. Keeps thoughts squarely on sex. Can cause unraveling and undoing.

Here are some correspondences for the astrological signs.

Astrological Sign	Symbol	Characteristics: How the Sign Causes the Planet to Act
Aries	♈	Is all about action. Causes impulsive actions focused on self. Creates new life. Leads or goes in its own direction. Is focused on identity. Is focused on the beginning and on getting started. Is brought to anger easily. Forgets that there are others. Represents courage, passion, and fervor. Is the pioneer. Can be summarized as "Here I come, get out of my way!" Is all about the being and doing.
Taurus	♉	Shows great persistence. Likes crafts. Is tied to the physical body. Can be stubborn. Likes to beautify. Is sensual. Likes to give and receive physical touch. Ensures and is concerned with sustainability. Gathers and values possessions. Is practical. Has lots of stamina and determination, as well as patience. Shows stability and is well grounded. Is focused on material things. Drives slow growth, but steady. Keeps track of assets. Can be heard saying, "Don't make changes too quickly!"

Astrological Sign	Symbol	Characteristics: How the Sign Causes the Planet to Act
Gemini	♊	Sees both sides of the picture. Connects opposites. Delves into abstractions and analysis of intellectual topics. Supports mental health healing. Helps in gaining awareness. Pushes for flexibility and change. Imparts understanding of the world around us. Inspires curiosity and inquisitiveness. Loves exploration. Is playful. Can go at great speed. Seems unfocused. Is all about communication and loves to talk to anyone and everyone: "Hi, let me tell you about it!"
Cancer	♋	The three most important things are emotions, emotions, and more emotions. All the feels. Protects people and the home. Provides a sense of safety and security. Is subjective. Puts emotion over the mind. Lacks intellectual perspective. Identifies with emotions, not thoughts. Is focused on family. Is intuitive and psychic. Is sensitive and nurturing. Provides emotional security.

Astrological Sign	Symbol	Characteristics: How the Sign Causes the Planet to Act
Leo	♌	Is regal. Is self-centered, yet open. Is awake and aware. Has an expansive personality. Needs to feel special and be validated by others. Is warm and generous, and this is sometimes driven by a need for approval. Takes the lead. Loves revelry. Is full of confidence. Does everything with a flourish. Seeks attention and wants to be at the center of it all.
Virgo	♍	Is the epitome of purity. Is always in service to others. Values and accomplishes order. Brings about the completion of earthly things, like harvesting. Brings health. Is very detail- oriented. Feels that "It is all in the details!" Is well-described by the terms analysis, precision, efficiency, and perfectionism. Personifies neat-ness. Fusses about the little things. Misses the big picture. Uses a thought-ful rather than emotional approach. Judges and criticizes, destructively or constructively, and always with empa-thy. Is focused on the physical.

Astrological Sign	Symbol	Characteristics: How the Sign Causes the Planet to Act
Libra	♎	Looks for balance and justice. Takes interest in and affects legal situations. Sees both sides of the picture and compromises to balance them out. Negotiates. Arranges. Is faultlessly objective. Is concerned about how actions affect others. Is unemotional. Seeks one-on-one relationships; feels incomplete in solitude. Likes to host.
Scorpio	♏	Is surrounded by mystery. Brings about transformation. Is full of desire, sometimes dark. Effectuates shadow work. Is very intense. Is symbolic of death and rebirth. Is sex incarnate; *la petite mort*. Is full of passion. Makes deep emotional connections. Both keeps secrets and reveals secrets. Experiences intense emotions, but may not always show them. Has a lot going on under the surface. Is only interested in depth and is never superficial. Has and uses a deadly sting when threatened.

Astrological Sign	Symbol	Characteristics: How the Sign Causes the Planet to Act
Sagittarius	♐	Seeks the truth. Has high aspirations. Loves fighting on the barricades for a cause. Has a motto of "Aim higher than you can reach, and you will accomplish much on the way." Defines the vision. Always stands up for independence. Has excellent foresight. Tends to see the big picture and miss details. Loves a good quest. Can be heard shouting, "Truth above all." Allows no compromises. Dislikes opposite viewpoints.
Capricorn	♑	Creates laws and societal structure. Uses achievement as the metric of self-worth. Lives a life filled with seriousness and responsibility. Respects chosen authority and authority recognized by self. Values and performs hard work. Is goal-focused and determined to succeed. Is full of ambition. Is driven. Seeks to be prominent. Is focused and practical.

Astrological Sign	Symbol	Characteristics: How the Sign Causes the Planet to Act
Aquarius	♒	Is ever the change agent. Is unconventional and values personal freedom. Is full of ideas and often expresses them in terms of abstractions. Sets, pursues, and focuses on group goals. Supports humanitarianism above all. Has and expresses utopian ideals. Can be impractical in pursuing goals. Demonstrates mental and not emotional engagement. Can be resistant to change driven by others. Uses a theoretical approach to solving problems. Is a visionary driven by ideology. Sees humanity mostly as a collection of groups, and identifies self with a group or groups. Makes the rights and workings of groups, especially group governance, their mission. Champions human rights.

Astrological Sign	Symbol	Characteristics: How the Sign Causes the Planet to Act
Pisces	♓	Has no ego; is simply a member of the group. Is full of compassion. Merges with the group, the Universe. Is the end of all things. Activates healing of emotional wounds. Brings about spiritual healing. Perceives and advocates that all connections are universal. Has faith. Understands and promotes understanding of relative truth. Is empathic. Possesses strong intuition. Believes in unification of all. Lives a life based in mysticism. Can see the strands of the web that connects humanity. Is dreamy.

Finally, here are some correspondences for the astrological houses.

House	Characteristics: Aspect of Life the House Affects
First house	Personal wants and needs. Starting a new personal journey of any kind. Appearance.
Second house	Income, immediate family, possessions (those you have, or those you wish to manifest). Interests and talents.
Third house	How you communicate, negotiate, and do public speaking. Family and neighbor relationships.

House	Characteristics: Aspect of Life the House Affects
Fourth house	Extended family as well as close family and friends. Your home and its ambiance. Where you plan to retire.
Fifth house	Time to party! What you do for fun; what you do for pleasure. Creativity. Romance and affairs, not committed. Gambling. Sex. Children. Feeling good. Libido, love, pleasure, happiness, joy.
Sixth house	Health, either physical or mental. Work and career. Relationship with boss, coworkers, and your team. Routine, everyday tasks.
Seventh house	Marriage. Relationship with your partner. Things you plan to accomplish together. Also relationships with business partners and enemies.
Eighth house	Community money and resources, taxes, inheritances. Death. Secrets and fears. Anything occult. Mysteries. The physical aspects of your relationship with your partner. Preparing for death, initiation, intuition, sixth sense, being psychic, magic, mystery, transformation.
Ninth house	Higher education. Long-distance travel. Spiritual development. Learning about and understanding the world. Clergy and religion.

House	Characteristics: Aspect of Life the House Affects
Tenth house	Profession. Reputation. Your standing in society. Furthering of career. Increasing ambition and motivation to work. Public speaking. Public life. Public reputation. How the world views you. Your successes and achievements.
Eleventh house	Wealth, prosperity, and abundance. Gaining fame. Hopes and wishes. Groups you belong to. Your friends, social groups, organizations, and what to achieve within them. Working as a part of a group or organization with shared ideals. Long-term goals.
Twelfth house	Incarceration. Spiritual enlightenment. Freedom. Skeletons in the closet. Karma. Working with the subconscious. Banishing nightmares. Secrets. Maintaining spiritual health. Psychic skills and experiences. Working through disappointment, sorrow, and grief. The meaning of life. Self undoing.

Knowing how to utilize and combine correspondences can be challenging at first, so I've included some examples of how to use astrological correspondences for spell casting. First of all, make sure that the planets mentioned for each type of spell are in a place where they will support your goal and that the planets in the house and sign mentioned are not going to wreak havoc with your spell. You can find the placements for a given time and place at www .astro.com or another site; use the birth chart creation section for the date, location, and time that you plan to perform the spell.

- If your spell is about your personal wants and needs or about starting a new personal journey of any kind, pick a few days and times when you could perform the spell. Then, for each, check what planets will be in the first house and make sure that they support your goal.

    - Say, for example, you find that only the moon is in the first house at one of your proposed spell times. While this is not a terrible thing, it is also not very strong. The moon is not action-oriented—it is dreamy, based in the past, and introverted. If you go further and check what sign the moon is in at that time and find that it is in Capricorn, you should probably choose another time. The moon in Capricorn can be very emotional about any small lack of achievement and can diminish your magic with energies focused on past failure instead of on future success.

    - The zodiac goes through the houses once every twenty-four hours. If you pick an earlier or later time in the same day, you will find different planets in different signs in the first house.

- If your spell requires considerable action, find out which planets are in the zodiac sign of Aries. Also, check what sign and house the planet Mars is in and make sure it is somewhere that will support your goal.

    - Say that you wanted to do your spell on June 21, 2025. You find that Saturn is in Aries and Mars is in Virgo. Saturn is a slow-moving planet, full of restraint and self-discipline, and it's most uncomfortable in the sign of Aries. Being in Aries can make Saturn move quicker than usual—this could work in your favor so that the magic you send out is not out of control. With Mars in Virgo, the bounding Mars energy becomes focused as always on doing, but doing it *right*. The Virgo placement also ensures that not only beginning the action, but completing it, will happen. You may notice that this, so far, did not include the house. So far, I've only chosen a day; this was sufficient to determine what planet is in Aries and where Mars is. Now, let's say the spell is going to be performed in San Diego, and you want to do it at 9:00 p.m. You find that Pluto is in Aquarius in the first house. If the action you want to make happen is in the area of social activism, changing laws or rules, or toppling a government, this is an excellent placement. If your magic needs action in a different, more personal area, this placement may not help, and it could possibly derail you by putting focus on personal actions for the greater good of society, rather than the more personal goal that you were wanting to take action on. If you instead can cast your spell at 10:00 a.m., you have Mars in Virgo in the first house, which will strongly support action and keep it focused on your personal wants and needs.

• If your spell is about your income, your immediate family, or your stuff (your possessions, either those you have or those you wish to manifest), check what planets are in the second house. Also, check what planets are in Taurus. Determine where Venus is. Ensure that those placements support your goal. For business ventures, also check what sign and house Mercury will be in at the time that you plan to cast your spell.

• If your spell has to do with how you communicate or an upcoming situation where you will need to negotiate by speaking well, check what planets are in the third house and what planets are in Gemini. Also, check where Mercury is.

- If your spell has to do with extended family, your home, or where you plan to retire, check what planets are in the fourth house. What planets are in Cancer? And where is the moon?

- If your spell has to do with libido, love, pleasure, joy, relationships other than marriage, creative hobbies, or having children, check out what planets are in the fifth house, what is in Leo, and where the sun is.

- If your spell has to do with personal health, either physical or mental, or with public health, check what is in the sixth house, what is in Virgo, and where Mercury is.

- If your spell has to do with your relationship with your partner, marriage, or things you want the two of you to accomplish together, check what is in the seventh house, what is in Libra, and where Venus is.

- If your spell has to do with sex, the physical aspects of your relationship with your partner, preparing for death, initiation, intuition, being psychic, magic, mystery, or transformation, check what is in the eighth house, what is in Scorpio, and where Mars and Pluto are.

- If your spell has to do with higher education, long-distance travel, spiritual development, or any aspect of learning about and understanding your world, check what is in the ninth house, what is in Sagittarius, and where Jupiter is.

- If your spell has to do with your profession, your reputation, your standing in society, furthering your career, increasing your ambition, or your motivation to work, check what is in the tenth house, what is in Capricorn, and where Saturn is.

- If your spell has to do either with wealth, prosperity, abundance, gaining fame, your hopes and dreams, the groups you belong to, your friends, social groups, or organizations you are in and what you want to achieve within them, check what is in the eleventh house, what is in Aquarius, and where Saturn and Uranus are.

- If your spell has to do with incarceration, spiritual enlightenment, freedom, the parts of you that only you know about, karma, working on your shadow, your subconscious, banishing nightmares, or your secrets, check what is in the twelfth house, what is in Pisces, and where Jupiter and Neptune are.

Timing Using Planetary Days

In the system of planetary days, each day as a whole is ruled by a planet. There is another system below that, where each hour of the day is governed by the same or a different planet. I will only cover the planetary day system here, as the correspondences of the planets for planetary hours are the same as for the planetary days.

Here are the rulers of each day of the week:

- Sunday: Sun
- Monday: Moon
- Tuesday: Mars
- Wednesday: Mercury
- Thursday: Jupiter
- Friday: Venus
- Saturday: Saturn

Here are some examples of using planetary days when scheduling your spell work.

- If you want to manifest wealth, be noticed by those in power, or make new friends, work under the influence of the sun.

- Work under the influence of the moon if you need to negotiate on behalf of your country or your company, need help with your divination skills, want to ensure safe and enjoyable travel, need to deliver messages in general, need to find your way (especially at sea), want to find love, or want to find positive emotion.

- If you are in the military and need to manifest success in war, further your military career, or be courageous when facing the enemy, work under the influence of Mars.

- If you want to improve your ability to communicate well, expand your intellect, improve divinatory skills, and ensure your business doesn't run into snags and delays, work under the influence of Mercury.

- To manifest prosperity in general, make new friends, have good health, and find joy in life, work under the influence of Jupiter.

- Work under the influence of Venus if you want to have safe travels or if you want to find love, friendship, or joy in life.

- If you want to talk to spirits of those who died naturally, bless a house or other building, see your business prosper, get your home in order, or learn new material quickly and easily, work during the influence of Saturn.

A Simple Method for Working with the Planets

Not only can you use the astrological placement of the planets to time your spell work, but you can also work directly with the planets, adding their power to what you send out.

Identify which planet will support what you want to attain. For example, Mercury works well for speaking engagements. The moon enhances psychic skills. Mars enhances drive and ambition.

After you've decided which planet you want to work with, find symbols and correspondences for that planet and adorn your altar with them. Add a picture of the planet. If your spell is written, include the symbol of the planet on the paper. If you are doing a candle spell, inscribe the candle with the symbol of the planet. (We'll talk more about those types of spells in chapter 9.)

Exercise: Planet Invocation

Invoking a planet means to pull the energy of the planet into yourself so that you can direct that energy into your spell. Read through this exercise and practice the devoking gesture before you start. Have something to eat and drink ready for grounding afterward.

You will need

A place to work undisturbed

An object holding a spell that you have already created, e.g., a paper spell or candle spell that you have not yet cast, or any other spell where you will use an object that you have created for this purpose

Hold the object you've chosen in your hands. First, inhale deeply into your diaphragm and exhale, creating an empty space. Ensure that your ego is not occupying that space. Then visualize the planet and pull the energy of the planet into you. You are filling yourself with the power of the planet.

Let this planetary energy flow from your core, out your hands, to the item holding your spell. With the power of the planet flowing out of your hands, trace the symbol of the planet on the object holding your spell. You can use your projective hand, an athame (magical knife), or a wand for this, or use your fingers to draw in the air.

Visualize the symbol you have drawn on the object shining brightly, then visualize it being brought into the object as the object absorbs the planetary power. This is powerful magic!

To devoke the planetary energy from your body, cross your arms in front of you and open up as if you were opening up a coat. Exhale and feel the power leave you.

Ground yourself by having something to eat or drink.

◆　◆　◆

As you can tell from this chapter, there are many factors to determining when the best time is to cast a spell in a given location. The phase of the moon, the placement of the planets, and the planetary days all play a part. There are also planetary hours, if you delve even deeper. It is rarely possible to get every one of these factors to line up in favor of your work. You want to find a location, day, and time that is reasonable, not one that is perfect. Sometimes, you don't have the luxury to plan this way, and you may have to work at a time that is not ideal for the purpose. In such a situation, to counteract any detrimental astrological influences, load your magic with as many layers as possible, as described in this book.

Part Two

))))●●●((((

MAGICAL BITS
AND PIECES

Chapter 4

))))●●●(((

SYMBOLS AND SIGILS

A symbol is a sign or object that represents something other than itself. If you send a heart in a message, the recipient will know that it means you are sending a message of love. In spell work, symbols are used because of the Law of Similarity. When a symbol is used in a spell, it is a stand-in for the goal that the spell is to manifest.

Male Symbol

One symbol can have multiple interpretations. The symbol for male also symbolizes the planet Mars and iron. While learned opinions vary, one explanation for this is that the symbol represents a shield and a sword. The shield and the sword were used mainly by men when the symbol was created.

Likewise, the following symbol for female, Venus, or copper is often interpreted to be a metal mirror, an item used more by women at the time the symbol was created.

Female Symbol

You see that some symbols are concrete in some way; they depict something that is closely related to what they represent. But other symbols are purely abstract, like this alchemy symbol for arsenic:

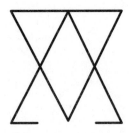

Alchemy Symbol

This chapter covers symbols and teaches you how to make sigils. Sigils are symbols that have inherent magical powers. These powers arise because the sigil is created with intent; the creator imbues the sigil with magic during the process of creation. Many sigils are mysterious looking to those who aren't initiated into its secrets. This is typically intentional so that the sigil will not get misused by those who were not invited to make use of it.

The Language of Symbols

Symbols exist everywhere in everyday life, and they, too, can be employed in magic. You can use the dollar sign ($) to manifest prosperity in countries that use the dollar as currency. You can use pictures or symbols for boats, trains, cars, or airplanes to manifest travel or speed, a cornucopia to manifest abundance, and so on.

This chapter will introduce some of the most commonly used symbols in spell crafting. Of course, there are many symbols used by witches and magical people. This chapter will discuss the ones that I come back to most often: the pentagram, the sun, the triple moon, the yin-yang, and the owl.

The Pentagram

The pentagram is a symbol with many meanings.

Occultism (e.g., the Hermetic Order of the Golden Dawn and Aleister Crowley's Thelema system) uses the pentagram as a central, magical symbol. The single point represents Spirit, and the double points represent the physical. For Crowley, the inverted pentagram represented Spirit descending to matter. In contrast, the Hermetic Order of the Golden Dawn considered the inverted pentagram evil, with the physical and mundane overtaking the spiritual.

In Christian times, the pentagram symbolized the five wounds of Christ.

In the Church of Satan, an inverted pentagram inscribed in a circle and depicting a goat's head is used as the registered logo and primary symbol of the religion.

Freemasonry also uses the pentagram. It is said that the symbol is often seen on Freemason regalia, yet is never mentioned in their texts.

The pentagram even has connections to mathematics. "According to Pythagoras, the five points of the pentagram each represent one of the five elements that make up man: fire, water, air, earth, and psyche (energy, fluid, breath, matter, and mind; also liquid, gas, solid, plasma, and aethyr, or spirit)."[3] That is a lot of correspondences in one sentence! You probably heard about Pythagoras in geometry class because of the Pythagorean theorem. Pythagoras made it clear that the pentagram does not stand for evil. In fact, it is a venerable symbol that has represented the elements, at least since around 500 BCE.

Drawing the Invoking Pentagram

Use the invoking pentagram to help manifest your spell. Draw the symbol in the air above the item that contains your spell.

Start with your hand above your head. Draw diagonally down to your left hip, diagonally up to your right shoulder, straight across to your left shoulder, diagonally across to your right hip, and back up to straight above your head. Make your movements as even as you possibly can. Finish by drawing a circle, seen clockwise from your perspective, that touches all the points of the pentagram.

---

3. "The Pentagram in Depth."

Invoking Pentagram

While you draw the pentagram, visualize magical power coming into the spell item through the pentagon that is formed in the middle of the pentagram.

Drawing the Banishing Pentagram

Use the banishing pentagram to help get rid of something. Draw it in the air and throw it at anything coming toward you that you do not want to reach you.

Banishing Pentagram

Start with your hand at the lower left hip. Draw diagonally to above your head, then down to your right hip, up across to your left shoulder, straight across to your right shoulder, and back down to your left hip. The banishing pentagram has no circle around it.

Practice drawing the invoking and banishing pentagrams. Have someone check that they are straight and even or practice in front of a mirror. These need to be second nature to you so that you do not have to think about how you draw them when the time comes to use them for magic.

The Triple Moon

The triple moon symbol shows three phases of the moon. On the left is the waxing crescent, in the middle is the full moon, and on the right is the waning crescent.

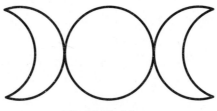

The Triple Moon

This symbol is receptive and is used in spell work to call in the power of the Goddess to help manifest the desired goal.

The Sun

The sun symbol is used to manifest male fertility, projective energy, vitality, ambition, and willpower.

The Sun

The Yin-Yang

The yin-yang symbol is used to create a balance of projective and receptive energies. It also can be used to balance opposites and ensures that opposites complement each other.

The Yin-Yang

The Owl

The symbol of the owl can be used to attain wisdom and insight. Owls are traditionally associated with knowledge, learning, and intelligence.

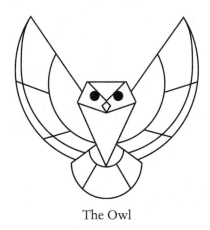

The Owl

Exercise: Finding Symbols

YOU WILL NEED

Access to the internet and a browser

A printer or paper and something to draw on the paper with, e.g., colored pencils

To practice your skills, pull up your favorite search engine online and search the word *symbol*. Look at the images. If you find some symbols that could be correspondences for a goal of yours, print them out or draw them. You can also use the symbols listed in this chapter.

Using the Tarot in Magic

There are many systems of symbols. Chapter 3 introduced some astrological symbols, for example. Another symbol system that is widely used in magic is the tarot. Tarot is a card deck that traditionally has seventy-eight cards. It has four suits that correspond to the four suits in a regular deck of playing cards, but there is an extra court card in each suit. These together constitute what is called the Minor Arcana. In a typical tarot deck, there is also a set of twenty-two cards in a trump suit called the Major Arcana. Each card in the tarot carries a different meaning, based on the symbols in the card. The symbols in the card and the corresponding interpretation can be used to layer magical spells.

Acquire or borrow a set of tarot cards if you do not already own one. You will need to set this deck aside for magical purposes for the next three months or so. If you are getting a new deck or borrowing one, please make sure that the pip cards (the cards ace through ten in the four basic suits) have actual pictures of something taking place, rather than images that simply reflect the number on the card. The Rider-Waite deck is the standard from which most fully illustrated decks are built. Many decks that descend from the Rider-Waite have beautiful and meaningful artwork, and any one of those are an excellent choice.

If acquiring a tarot deck is not possible for you, install a free tarot app on your phone if you can. The Galaxy Tarot app is excellent. If you cannot acquire a deck nor install an app, perform a search on the internet for "random tarot card" and find a site where you can draw a card every day.

Exercise: Tarot Symbolism

YOU WILL NEED

A tarot deck that has pictures on the pip cards. The deck
should be solely used for this exercise, which will last for
seventy-eight days. If you can't get a deck, you can use a
tarot app or website.

For the next seventy-eight days, draw one card per day. Then
examine the card art. Imagine that you are inside the scene that
the card displays. Take a good look around. Does what you see and
how it makes you feel align with success for any of your goals?

Look up the meaning of the card and determine whether the
standard interpretation supports any of your goals. If the card supports one of your goals in any way, put it aside to be used in a
future spell for that goal. If the card does not help with any of
your current goals, place it in a scrap pile for later use. Do not put
the card back in the deck, because you will continue to draw from
the deck until you have analyzed every card. This is a great way to
familiarize yourself with the symbols in tarot while you are collect-
ing correspondences for use in your magic.

Using the Runes as Symbols

The runes are an alphabet of symbols, much like the Greek alphabet, the Russian alphabet, and others. A letter is called a *runestave*.
Runes are a magical tool that can be used to manifest things, and
they are also a divinatory tool that can provide clarity in a situation.

There are several rune alphabets. The most widely used in
magic are the Elder Futhark, the Anglo-Saxon Futhark, and, occasionally, the Younger Futhark. I grew up in Sweden and learned the
Elder Futhark as an alphabet in school. Therefore, it is the type that

I work with. This section presents the Elder Futhark runes with their interpretation for use in magic.

Rune Symbol	Rune	Corresponding Letter	Meanings for Spell Work
ᚠ	Fehu	F	Use to manifest prosperity and generosity. Can also be used in religious magic along with offerings to the deity.
ᚢ	Uruz	U, V, O	Use to manifest strength, cope with difficult situations, gain energy, ensure good health, and increase libido.
ᚦ	Thurisaz	Th	Use to remove chaos: Draw the rune and cross it out or burn the paper with the intent of burning away the confusion or chaos. This rune can also be used as a magical defense. Thorns pointing outward are powerful protection.

Rune Symbol	Rune	Corresponding Letter	Meanings for Spell Work
ᚠ	Ansuz	A, AE	Use to enhance your career, for successful speaking engagements, to remove writer's block, or to remove analysis paralysis that is preventing you from reaching a decision.
ᚱ	Raido	R	Use to give extra power to your spells. Also use to symbolize travel and for safe and successful travel. This rune helps you take control of your circumstances and manifest your will and intentions. It is also suitable for intellectual undertakings.

Rune Symbol	Rune	Corresponding Letter	Meanings for Spell Work
ᚲ	Kenaz	K, Hard C	Use to remove disease or gangrene in your life, as this rune symbolizes disease and can be removed and burned. It is excellent for combating addiction, whether that is to drugs or alcohol, watching Netflix, or playing video games. Use to remove danger. Can also be used when working to gain new knowledge or when analyzing something to gain a deeper understanding. In the latter context, Kenaz works particularly well in conjunction with Ansuz.
ᚷ	Gebo	G	Use to offer devotion; ask for the development of the Higher Self in return—a gift exchange. Use to manifest balance in a relationship, perhaps between a seller and a buyer in a sale-purchase situation.

Rune Symbol	Rune	Corresponding Letter	Meanings for Spell Work
ᚹ	Wunjo	V, W	Use to manifest fulfillment and joy.
ᚺ	Hagalaz	H	Use with caution! This is a rune that can cause havoc if used carelessly. You can use it like Thurisaz and Kenaz: to remove danger.
ᚾ	Naudhiz	N	Use when you need to think outside of the box and to manifest a solution to any challenge you encounter.
ᛁ	Isa	I	Use to cause things to come to a halt or to preserve the status quo.
ᛃ	Jera	J, (Y)	This rune represents the harvest. Use to create positive and lasting change and to manifest the benefits of your hard work.
ᛇ	Eihwaz	Ï (Long e, pronounced as a separate vowel)	Use to release fear of death, for initiations, for protection, for astral travel, and for communication with the Norse gods.

Rune Symbol	Rune	Corresponding Letter	Meanings for Spell Work
Ƙ	Pertho	P	Use to remember past lives, reveal hidden answers, and increase luck.
Y	Algiz	Z	Use for protection.
Ƽ	Sowilo	S	Use to fortify other spells and for healing.
↑	Tiwaz	T	Use to get justice, find courage in frightening situations, and find the strength to sacrifice for others.
ß	Berkana	B	Use for all family and domestic matters and for healing women's issues.
M	Ehwaz	E	Use for safe travels and to finish what you have started.
M	Mannaz	M	Use to manifest the help of others and to bless group activities. Also, use for blessings that are for all of humankind.
Γ	Laguz	L	Use to enhance psychic powers, healing, inner awareness, and intuition.

Rune Symbol	Rune	Corresponding Letter	Meanings for Spell Work
ᛜ	Ingwaz	Ng	Use to bring a project to conclusion and to close the circle. Also use for fertility, especially male.
ᛞ	Dagaz	D	Use to get a fresh start and when making new resolutions.
ᛟ	Othilo	O	Use to protect heirlooms or your land, or to bless a gestating baby.

How to Use Runes in Spells

You can use runes as an alphabet and write out a word or words in the Runic alphabet. When doing this, you must consider what each rune stands for so that you don't have letters that contradict or lead to unexpected consequences; choose your word carefully so that the runes you use to write it out support your goal.

You can also choose individual runestaves that correspond to what you want to manifest without having them make up a word.

A common way to use runes in magic is to create bind runes, which involves combining multiple runes in one symbol.

Using the Runic Alphabet for Magic

Here is an example of using the runic alphabet as part of a spell for prosperity.

You write out the English word *prosperity* in the Elder Futhark. Rune magic prefers odd numbers, but *prosperity* has ten letters, an even number. So you add an extra e, creating the eleven-letter word *proseperity*. Then, you end up with the following runestaves:

- Pertho: Luck
- Raido: Ride or travel; being in control
- Othila: Inherited land or inherited genes; inheritance in general
- Sowilo: The sun; light on your path; divine support; defeat evil; victory
- Ehwaz: Travel and control; change for the better; continuing on the same path
- Pertho
- Ehwaz
- Raido
- Isa: Stability; preservation; stagnation; needing to freeze plans
- Tiwaz: Bravery; victory in battle; willpower
- Eihwaz: Go forth; aim high

There is a significant risk in this particular case, which is why I included it here so that you can see what to look out for. Including Othila may mean that the prosperity that you manifest will come through an inheritance.

Using Individual Runes as Symbols

Building off the previous example, let's consider another way to use runes in a spell for prosperity. Instead of writing out the word, you choose two runes that both represent prosperity and draw them as part of your spell.

- Fehu: Represents wealth
- Jera: Harvest time

This approach is, in this case, a safer way forward than the previous example of using the runes as an alphabet. In the case of using individual runes as symbols instead of letters, you choose the exact runes you want, helping to avoid unpleasant consequences.

Rune Prosperity Spell

YOU WILL NEED

Access to the rune chart earlier in this chapter, unless you already know the meaning of each runestave

Building off the previous example, where individual runes are used as symbols in a hypothetical prosperity spell, pick an appropriate third runestave to include. It is recommended to always use odd numbers when working with runes.

Creating Bindrunes

Bindrunes are often used in talismans and amulets. Amulets are protective, and talismans bring good luck, usually for a specific purpose. For safety and protection, always add Algiz at the ends of a bindrune, even if protection is not the primary goal of the bindrune.

Here are some examples of bindrunes that I have created in the past:

This rune represents elemental protection for the home and legacy; Othila and Algiz are in all four directions.

This rune represents elemental protection while traveling; Raido and Algiz are in all four directions.

This rune increases fertility for couples; it shows Ingwaz and Berkana with Algiz.

This rune is meant to ensure balance as things change; it includes Jera and Gebo with Algiz.

Exercise: Find Runestaves

You will need

Access to the rune chart earlier in this chapter, unless you already know the meaning of each runestave

Think about your goals. Choose one of your goals, then find one or three runestaves that will support that goal or strengthen your spell.

Divination Using the Symbolism of the Runes

Divination is a form of magic. Divination with runes uses the symbolism of each stave to discern the true nature of a situation and how best to proceed. Divination helps you determine what needs and concerns you should create spells for. This section describes a simple technique you can use to divine which issues you need to work on. You can use tarot cards instead of runes if you prefer.

Cut out twenty-four pieces of paper and draw one runestave from the Elder Futhark on each piece. Place them in a pile. Draw seven rune papers from the pile and lay them facedown in the shape of a pillar with the first-drawn on the bottom, building upward. Then draw seven more rune papers and create another pillar to the right of the first one, also facedown, so that you have seven pairs. Lay each piece with intent.

To interpret the rune papers, flip over the two rune papers that are at the bottom of the pillars. Make your way up the pillars as you read the corresponding paragraph.

The lowest pair of runestaves represents your right to live. The left runestave represents whether you are balanced and grounded. It also tells you what influences your current situation in regard to your safety, economic status, and emotional balance. It represents bodily health regarding your feet, hands, and digestive system. The right runestave shares guidance for how you can proceed to improve the situation.

The second-from-the-bottom runestaves represent your right to have a joyful life. The left stave shows you what is currently influencing your libido and sexuality, your emotional (but not romantic) connections to others, your creativity, and your ability to feel joy. It also answers questions about the health of your reproductive system. The right stave indicates what you need to do to improve the situation.

The third staves from the bottom represent your right to take action when needed. The left stave shows you what influences your ambition or lack thereof, your willpower, any addiction issues you have, and your moral character. It indicates if you have an overly dominant or submissive approach to life. Physically, it answers questions about back problems and obesity. The right stave shows you what you need to do to improve the situation.

The middle staves represent your right to love and to be loved. The left stave shows you what influences your love of self and your love of others, as well as any issues with codependency or clinginess. Physically, it shows you what influences any heart problems or lung problems that may be affecting you. The right stave shows you what you need to do to improve the situation.

The fifth staves from the bottom represent your right to communicate and to speak and be told the truth. The left stave indicates whether you have issues telling the truth, communicating clearly, or understanding what others are telling you and why. Physically, it shows what causes any throat, shoulder, or neck issues you may have. Again, the right stave shows you what you need to do to improve the situation.

The sixth staves from the bottom, the second from the top, represent your intuition, psychic abilities, and intellect. The left stave shows you what is going on with your ability to communicate with the dead and spirits, your divination abilities, your ability to see patterns, your ability to classify and learn new information, and your intellectual power. In terms of your body, it explains headaches, dizziness, and eye/vision issues. The right stave indicates what you need to do to improve the situation.

The seventh and final staves represent your spirituality. The left stave represents what is influencing your spirituality, your ability to connect with deity, and your own divinity. Physically, issues related to old age are shown here, especially those related to mental acuity. The rights stave shows you a way forward that will improve the situation.

Using Symbols in Magic

There are so many ways you can use symbols in your spell work. When you have found appropriate symbols to strengthen your spell, you can draw them on paper for paper spells, on candles for candle magic, or on any item that you are using in your spell. You can include printouts of the symbol, you can draw the symbol in the air using your finger, or you can craft the symbol out of clay, twigs, yarn, embroidery, or another material that your skills and interests lead you to. The important part is ensuring that the symbol is clear, aligned with your intent, and included when you cast the spell. If you're doing a spell in your office, having a printout or drawing in the bedroom next door will not do it.

Sigils: Personal Magical Symbols

A sigil is a symbol that has magical power. As an example, a bindrune is a sigil. A sigil is usually a unique symbol that comprises several other symbols or letters. I consider the ultimate authority on sigil creation to be Austin Osman Spare. His method for activating sigils differs from my understanding of magic, as it was based on how psychology was interpreted at that time; his ways of creating sigils, however, have stood the test of time.

To illustrate the various ways you can use sigils in your spell work, I will use the same example in each of the following methods. Let us say that you need a car that is reliable and legal, and you want to include sigils in your spell work to achieve this goal.

Method One: Starting from a Picture of the Intent

First, you draw a picture of a car with registration decals and a smile. The smile symbolizes that the car is working and reliable. Next, you stylize and simplify the image into a sigil. When using this method, you can and should use standard symbols, when they exist, as the starting point. Standard symbols are symbols that are understood to mean the same thing by many people, e.g., a picture of a mobile phone for communication and an airplane, car, or train for travel.

Method Two: Starting from a Written Affirmation of the Intent

This method starts with the goal stated as an affirmation, which is a statement in the present and positive. In this case, the affirmation is "I have a reliable and legal car." Write the affirmation in capital letters.

The next step is to pull the words together as one long word, removing any letters that appear more than once. Thus, you have "IHAVERLBNDGC."

Then, combine these letters into a symbol. The letters may be used upright, upside down, sideways, or even as mirror images. The result can be simplified and stylized to create a sign that is pleasing to the eye. Here is an example of a sigil that could be made from these letters:

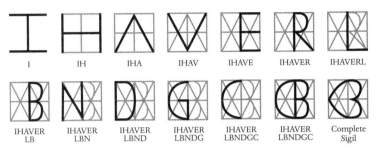

Process of Creating the IHAVERLBNDGC Sigil

While working on the sigil, keep the goal at the front of your mind. This will charge the sigil as you work.

Method Three: Using "As It Sounds" Spelling

How would you write out "I have a reliable and legal car" the way it sounds? Maybe as "AYEVEAREELIEYABEL NLEGULLCAHR."

Just like in method two, remove any duplicate letters: AYEVRLIBNGUCH.

You have just created a magical word! From here, you can either create a sigil as in method two, or you can use the word as-is in a spell.

Using Sigils in Spells

There are so many ways you can use sigils in spell work. Here are a few examples.

- Sigils can be drawn on amulets and talismans.
- Sigils can be drawn on candles for candle spells.
- Sigils can be drawn on paper (parchment is traditional) and handled in any of the ways a paper spell is handled.
- The magical word can be said as a magical incantation.

- You can use a sigil in any way you would use a symbol.

- You can create a sigil for your name (or your magical name, if you have one). Imbue the sigil with the intent that anything that you inscribe the sigil on is yours and remains yours forever. The sigil then becomes a spell for protection against loss or theft.

- You can inscribe a sigil on a clay amulet.

- You can find cross-stitch patterns for common symbols like the runic alphabet. These can be combined into bindrunes without too much trouble. For some symbols, you may be able to find a knitting pattern. If you are skilled at making patterns, you can create your own pattern for your sigil. Embroidering or knitting the sigil with intent, focusing on the goal as you create it, adds a great deal of magical layering power. You can then incorporate the embroidered or knitted item into a spell bag, sew it into a piece of clothing, or carry it with you.

Exercise: Create a Sigil

You will need

Pen and paper or a graphics program to work in

A Book of Shadows, grimoire, or magical notebook for
    documentation

Using any of the methods described above, create a sigil for a goal of yours. Or, if you'd prefer, create a sigil for your name.

)))）●●●((((

CORRESPONDENCES

A correspondence is an item or thing that is in some way associated with another item or thing, often by custom and tradition. Sometimes, there is an easily discerned connection or similarity between the items that correspond to each other, and sometimes there is not.

Correspondences work because of the Law of Similarity. Adding correspondences to a spell adds additional layers of power.

In this chapter, I will discuss some of the most common correspondences used in spell work.

Chakra Correspondences

The chakras are energy centers that exist in the subtle body, as opposed to the physical body of flesh and blood. You cannot see the chakras if you open up a body. This is because the chakras are not physical, though they have an active, energetic link to the endocrine system. Through that link, the chakras affect physical health. The chakras also have a powerful connection with the emotional state of a person and their personality.

Here are summaries of the seven main chakras:

Root Chakra: Located at the perineum. Corresponds to earth, the color red, identity, safety, grounding, stability, and the right to live and to be safe. An unbalanced root chakra can show up as an illness of the feet or legs; constipation; an eating disorder; hemorrhoids; fear and anxiety; poor eating habits; lack of exercise; lack of stability in life; difficulty manifesting goals; hoarding; hypochondria; and being overly materialistic. Heal with red crystals.

Sacral Chakra: Located below the navel. Corresponds to water, the color orange, sexuality, pleasure, feelings, connections with others, creativity, and joy in life. An unbalanced sacral chakra can show up as issues of the reproductive system; lack of libido or too much libido; being overly emotional or unfeeling; denying yourself pleasure or being addicted to fun and enjoyment; a lack of creativity or being too outside-of-the-box; and lack of joy in life. Heal with orange crystals.

Solar Plexus Chakra: Located at the solar plexus. Corresponds to fire, the color yellow, will power, action, drive, boundaries, and ambition. An unbalanced solar plexus chakra can show up as issues of the digestive system, including the gallbladder; being domineering or overly submissive; exhibiting a lack of limits and boundaries; lack of willpower; addiction; over-ambition; being excessively competitive; aggression; and being a workaholic. Heal with yellow crystals.

Heart Chakra: Located at the heart. Corresponds to air, the colors green and pink, love, self-love, relationships, and the right to love and to be loved. An unbalanced heart chakra can show up as issues of the heart and lungs; depression; inability to form friendships or loving relationships; fear of developing friendships or loving relationships; giving so much that you are neglecting yourself; and depending on someone else's happiness for your own (codependency). Heal with green or pink crystals.

Throat Chakra: Located at the throat. Corresponds to the color blue, communication, the ability to express thoughts and feelings, diplomacy, the right to be heard, and the right to speak and hear the truth. An unbalanced throat chakra can show up as issues with the throat, neck, or shoulders; an inability to express thoughts well; being tongue-tied; shyness; being unable to state desires or opinions; excessive talking without conveying anything; speaking too loudly; lying; or being unable to stay quiet when that is the best path to take. Heal with blue crystals.

Third Eye Chakra: Located in the center of the forehead, between and then above the brows. Corresponds to the colors indigo and purple, intuition, knowledge, wisdom, insight, psychic abilities, clairvoyance, judgment, contact with spirits, intellect, and the right to know. An unbalanced third eye chakra can show up as headaches or vision problems; being unrealistic; living in fantasyland; hallucinations; bad dreams; an overactive imagination; being overly analytical; being absent-minded; a blocked intuition; difficulty learning new material; needing everything spelled out explicitly; not being able to read between the lines; problems with general understanding;

diminished mental acuity; and cluelessness. Heal with purple or indigo crystals.

Crown Chakra: Located at the top of the head. Corresponds with the colors violet and white, connection with deity, the deity within, the Higher Self, nature, the Universe, and the right to experience the Divine. An unbalanced crown chakra can show up as feeling superior to others; feeling more connected to the Divine than anyone else; being holier-than-thou; being very dreamy and not grounded; being absent for a period of time; spacing out; an inability to connect with deity; not understanding your spiritual path; and not understanding your purpose in life. Heal with violet or white crystals.

Color Correspondences

One of the most common ways to work with color correspondences in magic is to use a candle, a piece of paper, or fabric in a color that matches your intent. For example, burning a pink candle while performing a love spell, or using green fabric in your healing poppet. Any way you can incorporate the color with intent will layer your magic and add power. Below are some common color correspondences, and in some instances, I also explain where those correspondences come from.

Crimson

- **Traditional:** For purification and to gain power; leadership; royalty.

- Use in spells that are for getting a promotion or for successfully stepping into a position of authority.

Scarlet, Red

- **Traditional:** Birth; warning; lust; war; anger.
- **Element-Based (Fire):** Enthusiasm; excitement; ambition; passion.
- **Chakra-Based (Root):** Grounding and stability.
- The element-based and the chakra-based correspondences appear contradictory. Stating the intent and clarifying which system is being called upon resolves that issue when casting a spell.

Orange

- **Traditional:** Radical transformation; getting attention; optimism.
- **Chakra-Based (Sacral):** Emotions; joy in life; libido.
- Use in spells to increase or decrease lust and desire as needed.
- Use in spells to find happiness in your current circumstances.

Yellow

- **Traditional:** Making a powerful impression; the sun.
- **Element-Based (Air):** Intellect; musicality; learning; analysis; memory.
- **Chakra-Based (Solar Plexus):** Will power; endurance; setting boundaries; ambition; action.

Pink

- **Traditional:** Love; self-love; babies: baby girls, baby boys (archaic); femininity.
- **Chakra-Based (Heart):** Love; compassion; relationships.

Green
- **Traditional:** Healing; calming; soothing.
- **Element-Based (Earth):** Prosperity; fertility; manifestation; abundance; stability; perseverance; stubbornness; in for the long haul.
- **Chakra-Based (Heart):** Love; self-love; compassion; relationships; can combat jealousy.

Blue
- **Traditional:** Tranquility; serenity; mystery; successful large corporations (so-called "blue chip companies"); spirituality; Mother Mary; royalty; success in commerce.
- **Element-Based (Water):** Healing; emotional healing; death; initiation; rebirth; compassion; emotions; a portal to the Underworld.
- **Chakra-Based (Throat):** Communication; eloquence; being heard; truth.

Indigo
- **Traditional:** Introspection; supernatural powers; lack of conventional boundaries.
- **Chakra-Based (Third Eye):** Intuition; extrasensory perception such as telepathy, clairvoyance, or clairaudience; ability to communicate with spirits; learning, wisdom, insight, and knowledge; concentration.

Purple
- **Traditional:** Royalty; wealth; luxury; power; leadership; being dignified; magic; wizardry; mysteries; spirituality.

- **Chakra-Based (Third Eye):** Intuition; extrasensory perception such as telepathy, clairvoyance, or clairaudience; ability to communicate with spirits; learning, wisdom, insight, and knowledge; concentration.

Violet

- **Traditional:** Humility; modesty; Mother Mary; devotion; spirituality.

- **Chakra-Based (Crown):** Spirituality; connection with deity; connection with the Higher Self, nature, and the Universe; experiencing the Divine and the divine self; understanding deity within; internalizing "You are God, and you are Goddess."

White

- **Traditional:** Purity; innocence; faith; virginity; simplicity; new leaf; fresh beginnings.

- **Chakra-Based (Crown):** Spirituality; connection with deity; connection with the Higher Self, nature, and the Universe; experiencing the Divine and the divine self; understanding deity within; internalizing "You are God, and you are Goddess."

- **Spiritual (Wicca):** The God; the Lord; projective energy; dispersion; masculinity.

Black

- **Traditional:** Sophistication; elegance; death; evil; fear; simplicity; the Underworld.

- **Spiritual (Wicca):** The Goddess; the Lady; receptive energy; absorption; femininity.

Gold

- **Traditional:** Wealth; masculinity; sophistication; prestige; power; recognition; success; winnings; luxury; glamour; the sun.
- **Spiritual (Wicca):** The God; the Lord; projective energy; dispersion; masculinity.

Silver

- **Traditional:** Elegance; sophistication; wealth; prestige; luxury; glamour; the moon; defeating vampires, werewolves, and other evil.
- **Spiritual (Wicca):** The Goddess; the Lady; receptive energy; absorption; femininity.

Color Magic

Whenever you have cast a spell that involves a color, continue to surround yourself with that color even after you've finished doing your spell. You will help your goal manifest in two ways: you will keep your focus on Acting in Accord, and you will boost the magic by further layering it.

There are many ways you can incorporate color magic. Add a splash of that color to your outfit. Add color magic to your accessories by wearing a scarf, a pair of socks, or jewelry in that color. Anything that you deliberately add in your chosen color will help you keep focused. Paint your nails in that color, if you use nail polish. Get a color-shifting lamp and keep it on the color until your goal has manifest. Burn candles in that color. Eat foods of that color.

Number Correspondences

Numbers can be used as symbols in your spell work. Here are the correspondences:

0: The contemplation before the beginning; the womb; the dark moon; risk-taking to succeed.

1: Unity; beginnings; the ego; the all—the source; winning; being first and best; manifesting.

2: Polarity; balance; connectedness; cooperation; direction; emerging or deep spirituality.

3: Stability; truth; deity; the triple goddess; the Christian trinity; family: mother, father, and child; depth; fertility.

4: The four elements; the four cardinal directions; the circle; organization; balance and stability; security; the passage of time.

5: Creation and destruction; death and rebirth; transformation that brings change for the better; spirit over the mundane (remember the pentagram with spirit as the top point); power or power struggle; learnings; teachings.

6: Pleasure; joy; sex; marriage; carpe diem; temptations; making choices based on values.

7: Magic; everything psychic; surprises; pursuit of dreams; moving forward; sticking to it; difficult choice to take action, then movement.

8: Management; your way of making a living; your interests; how you spend your time; courage; the power of belief; success from trusting your abilities; consequences, good and bad.

9: Leadership; benevolent power; lighting the way for others; nearing the goal.

10: Completeness; the end; fulfillment; new beginnings on the horizon; tying up loose ends to be able to move on; completion means something else is now to come.

11: Instinct; intuition; trust; spiritual connection between you and others; karma and consequences.

13: Complete group; coven; Jesus and his disciples; Arthur and the knights of the round table (in some versions of the story); the sun and the twelve constellations.

22: Divine support; connection with the Divine; knowing the divine within; the divine self.

Say that you want to cast a spell to feel more joyful in your marriage, so you want to incorporate the number six in your magic. If you are adding sprigs of herbs to your spell, use six sprigs of one kind or one sprig each of six different kinds. If you are adding essential oils, use six drops of one kind, or one drop each of six different kinds. If you are writing a word on a paper spell, write it six times, or write six different words. If you are drawing a picture on the paper spell, repeat it six times, or draw six different pictures. Any way you can think of to incorporate the number six with intent will layer your magic and thus enhance its power.

Exercise: Number Correspondences
You will need
Access to the number correspondences in this chapter, unless you already know the meaning of each

Think about your goals. Choose one of your goals, then determine a number correspondence. Figure out how you could use that number correspondence in your spell work.

Herbs and Food Correspondences

Herbs and other foods can be used to layer many types of spells, so knowing the correspondences and magical properties of a few that you may already have on hand is very useful. Herbs and foodstuffs are also suitable for adding a quick intent to a meal that you are cooking. Say that you are going to do divination in the afternoon. Incorporating bay leaf and peppermint with intent into a light lunch will enhance your afternoon performance. Here are some other correspondences:

Apples can be used in spells to draw love and for health. "An apple a day keeps the doctor away" is actually magic.

Avocados are a potent aphrodisiac. Use to enhance your libido.

Bananas are, of course, phallic, and therefore enhance both male libido and male fertility.

Basil is used primarily for love and can also be used to manifest prosperity.

Bay leaves are used to enhance divination skills, clairvoyance/clairaudience, and other psychic talents. Burn bay leaves as incense while scrying. Bay leaves are also strongly protective and healing.

Beet juice, made by putting a beet in a blender and straining, can be used as a substitute for blood if you ever find a spell asking for blood. (You won't find any such spells in this book!)

Blackberries come from a plant that produces profusely and is challenging to get rid of. Therefore, they are a symbol of tenacity, so you can use them in spells for endurance. Because they are so abundant, they are also a symbol of wealth, so use them in any spell for prosperity.

Caraway seeds protect your items from being stolen. Keep a few seeds in your wallet! When worn or sprinkled in the home, caraway seeds also protect against evil spirits and negative energy. They protect against unwanted visitors and burglars when scattered around the perimeter of a property. If you are making a love potion, add caraway to ensure faithfulness.

Carrots are phallic and thus an aphrodisiac and can be used to enhance libido.

Cashews bring great wealth to those who grow them and are therefore a symbol of prosperity. Use in any spell for prosperity.

Celery stalk is phallic and an aphrodisiac and thus can also be used to enhance libido.

Cherries are heart-shaped and are therefore used to draw love.

Chili powder is hot and therefore protective. Sprinkle around the perimeter of your property to keep out anything that is not welcome. You can also add chili powder to any potion to draw love if you wish to add erotic heat.

Cinnamon is very magical! It connects you with the Divine when you burn it as incense or when used in potions or amulets. It is also healing and supports clairvoyance and any kind of divination.

Cloves are for prosperity. Crush cloves and burn them on a charcoal dish. Doing this also cleanses the space and is protective.

Coriander (cilantro) has many uses. Add fresh leaves or ground seeds to warm milk and honey, or add the ground seeds to warm wine (you can sweeten it with honey), as an aphrodisiac. You can crush the seeds and add to other prosperity herbs for a tremendous money-drawing incense. Carrying the seeds in a pouch brings healing.

Cucumber is healing.

Cumin is similar to caraway in many of its magical properties. It protects against theft when contained within an object. Cumin drives away evil spirits; therefore, you can use it for house cleansings. Cumin promotes fidelity.

Dried mushrooms are associated with the element of earth. They can be used in prosperity spells and fertility spells.

Fennel strengthens your mind and your ability to communicate and to convince. It assists with divination. It also enhances eyesight. It protects your privacy and helps keep you from unwanted contact with government agents, e.g., police or the tax authorities. Grow fennel around your home for privacy and protection. Hang dried fennel in your windows and doorways to protect your home from evil spirits; replace regularly.

Figs are good for male fertility and virility. You can also use them to sweeten a honey jar, described in chapter 9.

Garlic is sacred to Hekate. Offer garlic and bread and occasional pieces of cooked fish if you are asking for Her assistance. Garlic has strong healing properties. Garlic is protective, so wear a clove in a bag around your neck or place it over your door to keep unwanted spirits, undesirable visitors, and burglars away. Garlic is well-known for its ability to protect against energy vampires. It is also an aphrodisiac, though use it cautiously—some people cannot stand the smell or taste of garlic.

Ginger enhances the power of any spell. It lends raw power and speed to all magic. Eat crystallized ginger or pickled ginger (sushi ginger) before performing a spell, or sprinkle powdered dried ginger in a sachet to add power to your working. Grate 2 Tbsp of raw ginger into 1½ cups of water and boil for fifteen minutes, then add honey. Drink to enhance your magical power or mix with wine (can be nonalcoholic) for a potent love potion and aphrodisiac.

Grapes, whether fresh or in the form of raisins, are used to enhance fertility. They are also effective in drawing wealth.

Leeks protect you from many things, including weight gain. They are mildly diuretic. Because of their phallic form, leeks are used for fertility. They are also very protective.

Lemons can be used to cleanse objects energetically. Mix lemon juice with water and wash items with the mixture. You can also let lemon peel steep in water and use the water for energy cleansing. Put cut-up lemons in bathwater for the preparation bath before a ritual (more about this in chapter 8). Mix lemon with honey and hot water to cure a cold. You can even use a lemon as a poppet!

Eat **lettuce**. Wrap lettuce leaves in paper towels and place them under your pillow for a good night's sleep.

Lime has the same uses as lemon.

Marjoram is a fabulous herb that draws love and prosperity. It is also protective if you carry it in a sachet as an amulet.

Mint leaves can be used to relieve headaches, especially when mixed with rose leaves; rub the mixture on your temples and forehead. Make mint tea or a drink with mint as an aphrodisiac. Mix 1 Tbsp of lemon juice with ten mint leaves (muddle the leaves or grind the leaves before adding the lemon juice), then spread the mixture on your face to combat acne and to brighten your skin. If you have Fuller's earth clay (Multani mitti) at home, mix 1 Tbsp of the clay with a dozen ground mint leaves, ½ Tbsp of honey, and ½ Tbsp of plain yogurt, then use as a face mask for clear skin; put it on with intent and say an appropriate incantation for improving skin clarity, and leave on for twenty minutes before rinsing off. Keep a few mint leaves in your wallet to draw prosperity. Use sprigs of mint and rosemary to asperge Pagan holy water around the house as part of a house cleansing ritual. Mint is a catalyst for magic, so keep it on your altar during magical workings.

Nutmeg can be put to good use in prosperity spells. Sprinkle ground nutmeg as incense and add nutmeg to the envelope or container for your spell. If you are burning paper, sprinkle nutmeg on the fire as the paper burns.

Oats are another kitchen staple that draw prosperity.

Olive oil can be used as an anointing oil. Draw an encircled pentagram on the forehead of ritual participants as a blessing after you cast the circle and before you do any magical working. Also, use as an anointing oil for healing. Eat olives as an aphrodisiac.

Onion is used to draw sickness and negative energies out. Select an onion and cut it in half, then place one half under the bed of anyone who is sick or in any way afflicted; throw the onion away in the morning or, even better, bury it—do *not* eat it!

Oranges have many uses. Oranges can draw love and prosperity. Wine that dried orange peel has steeped in is a love potion and an aphrodisiac.

Papaya is for love! The seeds are slightly peppery, with a flavor reminiscent of nasturtium seeds. The pepperiness means that the seeds are protective and also lend power to any spell. You can eat a few seeds while performing a spell for extra power or add the seeds to the spell itself.

Parsley is an aphrodisiac, and you can also use parsley in fertility spells. Put some parsley in your preparation bath before a ritual for purification.

Peaches are sweet and fuzzy and bring sweet love. They also bring wisdom.

Pears are also sweet and bring sweet love. Share a pear with your partner as an aphrodisiac.

Pecans are good for prosperity spells.

Pepper is used for banishings and protection. Black pepper and white pepper are rejecting, though not as strongly as chili pepper, cayenne pepper, jalapeno pepper, and the like. Use black pepper together with salt to ward your property against evil; spread the mixture around the perimeter.

Peppermint enhances psychic powers and ensures sound sleep. Use it for purification as well. Put peppermint essential oil on cotton balls to keep mice away.

Pineapple juice can temper your libido and dampen lust.

Pistachios counteract any love spell that someone may have put on you.

Pomegranate is a fruit of transformation. Add pomegranate seeds or juice to any spell that is supposed to manifest a significant life change.

Potatoes can be used as poppets. Decorate the potato with a face. Use toothpicks for arms and legs, a tuft of parsley for hair, or matchstick heads for eyes. Be creative.

Raspberries are sweet and pretty, and as a result, they draw love.

Rice is another very magical kitchen staple. Carry rice in a sachet to ward off evil. Use in prosperity spells. It is okay to use raw rice outside. It is a myth that birds are harmed by uncooked rice, so go ahead and place some rice on your roof for protection against misfortune.

Burn sprigs of **rosemary** and carry them around the house during a house cleansing. Also, burn rosemary before any magic to clean away negative energies. It also ensures good sleep when put under a pillow or in a pillowcase and is protective during rest. Use rosemary in your preparatory bath before any ritual as an energy-cleansing agent. Rosemary can also be used in love spells, as an aphrodisiac, and for healing. Rosemary is an excellent substitute for **frankincense**. If you have a recipe that asks for frankincense and you have none, use rosemary instead. Rosemary is a powerful energy cleanser.

Saffron is a love substance. Use it in spells to draw love to you and as an aphrodisiac. Because of its expense, it is also potent in prosperity spells. Make a weak infusion of saffron and drink it before any kind of divination, as it enhances psychic powers; this tea also helps prevent sorrow and sadness.

Salt is cleansing. It is "energetic Clorox," so use with care. It will remove all energies, both positive and negative.

Sesame seeds are an aphrodisiac, and they are also helpful in prosperity spells. They can also reveal what is hidden and open doors that have been closed to you. Use in spells to manifest new opportunities and remove barriers.

Strawberries, like many berries, are sweet and pretty and therefore draw love.

Burn **tea leaves** as an incense for prosperity and add the leaves to any container you use for a prosperity spell. If you are burning paper in a prosperity spell, sprinkle black tea leaves on the fire for added power to the spell.

Thyme is a powerful healing herb. Burn it as an incense while performing healing spells and other healing work. Use thyme as a sleep aid by burning it at bedtime; you can also place thyme under a pillow or in the pillowcase. Burn thyme before divinatory work to enhance psychic powers. Burn thyme to cleanse during house clearings and before ritual and magical workings.

Turmeric is purifying. Add turmeric to Pagan holy water, but only if you are going to use it outside—turmeric stains badly.

Vanilla enhances libido and draws lust.

Exercise: Food Magic

You will need

Access to your kitchen cabinet

Pen and paper to document your findings

Think about your goals. Choose one of your goals, then find something in your kitchen that supports that goal. Think about how you could use that correspondence in your spell work.

Flower Correspondences

Adding fresh flowers or plant parts to your spells is powerful, and many find it incredibly satisfying. I will only include a few flowers and plants here, as this is a vast field in itself. I have included those that you might already have growing in a pot at home or in your garden, as well as flowers that you can easily find at a store. Think of this list as a start!

Remember that not all of these flowers are edible. Just because it is not listed as toxic in this list does *not* mean that you can ingest it. I have specifically pointed out a few that are edible. Always do your research before ingesting anything.

I also want to note that this list is for flowers and plant parts that you can use to layer paper spells and other spells where the spell materials will be discarded in some way. Fresh plant parts decay! So, for example, you should not use flower correspondences in spell work that needs to sit on your altar for several weeks.

Aloe vera is easy to care for, so if you are in a caregiving situation where you need things to get easier, this is a good plant to incorporate. Aloe vera is generally used for healing, emotions, and protection in spells because of its natural healing properties for rashes and burns. Because it is good for the skin, it is used in spells that enhance beauty.

Amaryllis is a symbol of beauty, so it is suitable for putting on a beauty glamour, i.e., any spell that makes you look especially attractive. Amaryllis is toxic, so do not ingest it.

Apple blossom is used for seeking fame. If you are working on a project but you aren't getting credit for it, use apple blossom in a spell to enhance your visibility.

Arborvitae means "Tree of Life." It lives for an almost unfathomably long time, sometimes over one thousand years. Because of this, it is a good plant to use in spells for longevity and good health. The wood repels termites, and it can therefore be used in spells against pests. Traditionally, it is also used for making friendships last. Arborvitae is an irritant, so do not ingest it.

Azalea is for moderation in all things. Use azalea in spells to temper overindulgence in anything, be it food, alcohol, gambling, computer games, or anything else. This plant is toxic—do not ingest.

Bougainvillea, when in a climate and soil that it prefers, is very difficult to kill. Thus, it is good to use in spells for endurance and also in spells for longevity. It flowers profusely, and because of this, it works well in prosperity spells. Its beauty brings a smile to almost every face, and therefore it is associated with joy. Its beauty tends to inspire awe and can bring back belief in magic.

Cactus is protective, thanks to having spines. Like mirrors, they can be placed in each cardinal direction in the home to keep anything with hostile intentions out.

Chamomile is soothing and calming. Use in spells to combat insomnia or nightmares. You can grind up the flowers and use them as incense for good sleep. If you have access to organic dried or fresh chamomile, you can make an infusion. You can also buy tea bags to make chamomile tea. A strong infusion also subtly lightens hair's blond shades when used as a rinse.

Carnations are healing and protective. Some people are allergic to the leaves, so you may need to use gloves. The flower petals are safe to eat if not sprayed with pesticides and not colored with unknown substances.

Chrysanthemums are protective. They also lift your mood and help you combat negative thinking. Use mums in spells to help dispel false beliefs about yourself.

Crocus brings joy in spring, of course, and can also be used in love spells. Because they come so early in the spring, they can be used to bless new undertakings. Forsythia can be substituted. Note: autumn crocus, which is not an actual crocus, is highly poisonous. Many true crocuses are toxic as well, so do not ingest.

Echinacea is a magical catalyst and strengthens spells. Add fresh or dried Echinacea to any spell to increase its power.

Geraniums are protective. They are exceptionally protective against negative self-talk. Use in spells to improve self-confidence and your view of yourself. They easily grow from cuttings; before you know it, you will have a house full of them. Therefore, they are also a symbol of fertility and prosperity.

Hibiscus increases libido. Hibiscus tea is readily available as tea bags, though it is rather tart. You can also use the dried flowers in love spells.

Hyacinths bring joy! They also promote restful sleep and prevent nightmares. The best way to use hyacinths is to have them potted in the room where you are performing the spell. The bulbs contain an irritant, so handle with gloves only. Do not ingest.

Lantana is a hardy plant and can be invasive in some areas. Because of this, lantana can be used in spells for stamina, endurance, or resilience. Lantana is easy to grow and therefore is good for prosperity spells. It is also stunning, so if your goal is to improve the looks of your home or yourself, lantana is an excellent choice to incorporate in your spell. Note that lantana is toxic to humans and can be fatal to animals. Don't ingest!

Lavender is for love. It also brings calm, peace, and restful sleep. Put dried lavender in a pillowcase. Its scent helps lift the mood and can help combat depression and sorrow. Cast a joy spell on a lavender sachet and keep it in your pocket; lift it to your nose to inhale the fragrance every so often to feel a sense of contentment and satisfaction during the day. Lavender is also cleansing and purifying.

Lilacs reject evil. This is an excellent plant to have at the edges of your property. Because they bloom for a very short time, they are good to use in spells that you wish to be active only for a short duration or for something that you want to manifest only for a short time. For example, if you wish to cast a spell to manifest a trip but are worried that it will backfire and end up with you moving, add lilacs to the spell to reinforce that the journey is time-limited.

Nasturtiums are very versatile! If you pick the flowers and bite the thin end, you can suck a small amount of nectar out of each one. Knowing this, you can use the flowers in any spell that needs sweetness, like honey jars. The flowers are edible and can be incorporated into salads unless pesticides have been used on them. In Victorian floral language, the flower stands for conquest. If using nasturtium to represent conquest, do so with caution, as it can backfire if you are not precise when phrasing your spell. Nasturtium can also help the absent-minded professor type, the person who neglects both their emotional and their physical self for intellectual pursuits. The leaves, which are also edible, resemble shields in shape, so they can be used to shield yourself or your property, according to the Law of Similarity.

Tulips are for always having enough and for good luck.

Oil and Fragrance Correspondences

Essential oils carry the same magic as the plant from which they were pressed. Not all essential oils come from herbs, spices, or other foodstuffs that we use in the kitchen; many oils come from fragrant plants.

Incenses are made from parts of plants, e.g., spices, herbs, flowers, ground seeds, essential oils, crushed resins and gums, ground wood, ground bark, or ground roots. Incenses have the same magical properties as the plants or trees from which they were made.

In this section, I will list a few oils and incenses that are good to have on hand, as well as their correspondences.

Cedar is cleansing, purifying, and protective. Cedar draws money and is therefore excellent for prosperity spells. Cedar assists in establishing sacred space, enhances the sixth sense, supports divination, and enhances magical power.

Clary sage (*Salvia sclarea*) is not the same plant as common or garden sage (*Salvia officinalis*). Clary sage is purifying and relaxing, and it lifts the mood. It brings clarity and aids in clairvoyance and clairaudience. It also supports intuition and connection with spirit. It can help you gain clarity about your path.

Copal is purifying and also draws love. Its fragrance is sweet, so you can burn it and waft some smoke into a honey jar just before you close it. Blend copal with frankincense and myrrh for an exquisite incense to purify your magical space and amplify the power of your spell workings.

Dragon's blood is a red resin from one of several types of trees. It is protective. It is excellent for house clearings as it drives away negativity and anything evil. It is a magical catalyst and enhances the power of other incenses and oils.

Frankincense, like dragon's blood, drives away negativity and anything evil. It elevates personal resonance with the Divine. Use frankincense to create sacred space. Frankincense is common in incense blends used in the Catholic church.

Jasmine attracts love, especially nonphysical love. It enhances elegance, poise, and gracefulness and creates prosperity.

Musk is an aphrodisiacal scent, first and foremost, and thus draws lust and passion. It helps balance your inner male and female aspects and supports the sacral chakra.

Myrrh is purifying and healing. It enhances the magic of other incenses and fills a space with comfort and peace. It provides connection with the Divine and creates an otherworldly and ethereal atmosphere for magical practices in both a mundane and spiritual sense.

Patchouli promotes prosperity and fertility, properties that often go hand in hand. It also draws love and lust. Like its cousin mint, it also is a catalyst for magic.

Pine is healing. Burning pine needles is purifying. You may want to keep some needles from your Yule or Christmas tree, if you have one, to use throughout the year. Pine is also associated with fertility and with prosperity.

Rose clears headaches. In magic, it is also used to draw love and to enhance beauty.

You may wonder why I did not list the very popular Nag Champa. Nag Champa is a wonderful fragrance, but it is a blend, and there is no standard for it. The exact ingredients vary by manufacturer, so there is no way of saying with certainty what the magical properties of a particular Nag Champa blend are. If it is your favorite scent and you wish to use it as the scent you use for all magical work, that will work fine. No Nag Champa blend that I am aware of has anything that inhibits magical workings, and repeatedly using it will put you in the proper magical mindset, which enhances your powers.

Aroma Magic

Another way to layer your magic and keep yourself focused is to surround yourself with the fragrances that support your goal. Add any herbs you used in spell work to a charcoal disc or boil a small pot of water on the stove with the herbs added as a potpourri.

You may already have some essential oils on hand that you use around your house. When you use an oil diffuser, your home gets filled with that magic, so you should use it! When you add oil to a diffuser, do so with the intent to manifest a goal that is supported by the oil you are using. If you performed a spell using herbs, you can add the essential oils of the herbs you used.

You can buy Bach Flower Remedies and drop them on your tongue. They are quite expensive, though. If regular stick incense exists for your fragrance of choice, that is an easy and quick way to add the scent to your life instead.

You can also add essential oils to 70 percent isopropyl alcohol (or higher) and keep it in a spray bottle to use as hand sanitizer. If you need to use a mask, you can spray the inside of your mask lightly with the same spray. Let it dry thoroughly before you put the mask on. Now your face cover will smell lovely!

You can also make oils to anoint yourself with while visualizing a goal being manifest. Mix the essential oils with a carrier oil and rub them on your wrists, like a perfume. Add a total of thirty-five drops of essential oil to ten mL of carrier oil in a roller-ball bottle and shake well. Shake before each use. If you make a considerable amount, add some vitamin E oil, as this helps preserve the mixture.

When you mix oils to wear, it is good to consider their scents in addition to their magical properties. If you are going to wear an oil, you want something that smells pleasing. The science behind achieving a pleasant smell when making a fragrant oil blend is the same as for making perfume: use a fresh, light, and vibrant top note to give a first impression of the fragrance. The top note dissipates rather quickly. Any citrus oil makes a good top note, as do ginger and mint.

Use a slightly heavier and more complex middle note to step in when the top note fades. Good middle note oils are cinnamon, lavender, clary sage, rose, jasmine, and rosemary. Clary sage and lavender are sometimes classified as top notes.

Use a calming bottom note that lingers on the skin and gives a lasting impression of the overall fragrance. Good bottom notes are vanilla, musk, frankincense, and patchouli.

Chapter 6

))))●●((((

THE FOUR ELEMENTS

T he four elements are not hocus pocus. The elements were documented in the Vedas as far back as 400 BCE, and possibly thousands of years before that.[4]

Each element is associated with a cardinal direction: north, east, south, or west. I work with the elemental directions according to their astrological placement. However, even in astrology, there is more than one way to associate the seasons with the elements. I follow the approach described by Mike Nichols.[5] In this approach, the fixed sign of the season—the sign in the middle of the season—anchors the season and determines its element.

---

4. "Of Religion by Discernment."

5. Nichols, *Re-Thinking the Watchtowers*.

In my practice, earth is in the east, with fire in the south, water in the west, and air in the north. Many practitioners work instead with earth in the north and air in the east. Practitioners who work in a circle call in the elemental energies from the cardinal direction associated with the element in their practice. Choose whichever approach feels right to you.

The elements are each associated with a family of beings termed *elementals* who carry and are made up of elemental energy but are also substantial. Each element has its own type of elemental, and each family has many subtypes.

The energies of the elements need to be present for a goal to manifest on the physical plane. In this chapter, I will explain the four elements in detail so that you can find appropriate correspondences for your spell work.

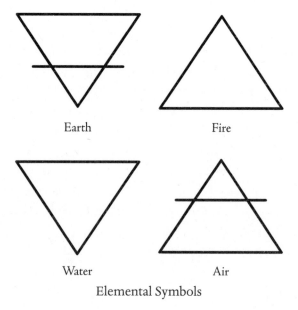

Earth   Fire

Water   Air

Elemental Symbols

The male elemental symbols, air and fire, are both phallic, pointing upward. The female elemental symbols are receptacles, receptive. This is not a coincidence. Also of interest is that the two elements that nearly all magical traditions put in the same places—fire in the south and water in the west—have no crossbar. This is an easy way to remember which symbol is which. The two elements that some magical traditions place in different directions (air and earth) both have crossbars. There is no great significance to this that I know of, but it is very helpful when trying to learn which symbol is which.

Earth

The earth element is the abundant and fertile Goddess or the growing earth. It is associated with spring, the morning, and new beginnings.

The spring season is anchored by Taurus, which is an earth sign.

The earth element is in the east and has receptive energy.

The earth elemental beings are the gnomes. The typical gnome is grounded and short and stout. Gnomes work with gemstones and precious metals. Elves, tree-sprites, brownies, and forest spirits are also of the Gnome family.

Use items symbolic of earth anytime your magic is about manifesting objects, items, and things that nouns can describe. The pentacle plate is the traditional tool. Other items representing earth are soil, salt, seeds, crystals, drums, coins, and shields. Most mammals represent the earth element as well.

Earth represents items, stability, foundation, grounding, security, steadfastness, manifestation, nurturing energies, prosperity, fertility, and budding life. Earth also represents the things in life that you need, the tangible things you touch, like food, clothes, and consumable goods.

Deities are whole and holy, while elemental energies are very one-dimensional and focused. Still, some gods are more of the earth element than others. Fertility deities like Demeter, Frey and Freya, the Vedic earth goddess Pritivi, and the Greek primordial earth goddess Gaia have strong associations with the earth element.

The pentacle is the tool that is used to bring energy into this realm from the other side.

The color correspondence for the earth element is green.

Fire

The summer season is anchored by Leo, which is a fire sign.

The fire element is in the south and has projective energy.

The fire elementals are the salamanders, which are either lizard-like, a fiery ball, or a humanlike creature licked by flames.

Use items that represent fire if your magic is about manifesting actions or passion. The wand is the traditional tool, though in some traditions, it is the athame (magical knife) or the sword. Other items representing fire are candles, lanterns, salamanders, brooms, staffs, hookah, liquor, all manners of phallic objects, rattles, sistrums, oils, perfumes of all kinds, things that ignite passion, braziers, and actual fire. Creatures—mythical and real—associated with fire include dragons, fire ants, salamanders, snakes, and the phoenix.

Fire represents action, passion, ambition, desire, drive, power, instinctual acts, zest, zeal, enthusiasm for tasks, bravery, ferociousness, and gusto. Fire also represents the things in life that you do, like sports and exercise.

Hestia, the Greek goddess of the hearth, is associated with fire, as are Helios the sun god, the Celtic Bride, and the Hindu fire god Agni.

The wand is the tool used to direct fire energy into a receptive object. For example, the wand would direct energy into the pentacle when using the pentacle for manifestation. Use the wand to effect change, make your plans come to fruition, change habits, and infuse passion.

The color correspondence for the fire element is red.

Water

The fall season is anchored by Scorpio, which is a water sign.

The water element is in the west and has receptive energy.

The water elementals are the undines, which are humanoid and fluid. Merfolk and river, lake, and ocean nymphs are all of the undine family.

Work with things that represent water when your magic is about emotions, death and initiation (and therefore rebirth and transformation), divination, or healing. The chalice is the traditional tool. Other representations of water are mirrors, goblets, seashells, mermaids, wine, glass, divination tools of all sorts, potions, rain sticks, bubbles, and representations of the moon. Fish, mollusks like oysters and mussels, starfish, frogs, dolphins, whales, and turtles also represent the water element.

Water represents emotions, healing, compassion, intuition, psychic powers, and change. Water also represents the things you feel in life, like anxiety, joy, happiness, love, and sadness.

Some deities closely associated with water are Poseidon, the Greek god of the ocean; Varuna, the Vedic god of water; Njord, a Norse god of the sea; and Aegir, who in Norse myth personifies the sea.

The chalice is the tool used to connect with others, directly communicate with deity, and see through the veil to contact spirits. Use the chalice in potions for healing, divination, and connecting with your loved ones. In formal rituals, water is combined with salt and used to bless the circle and the participants with the elements of earth and water through asperging. In some rituals, water is used as a blessing by drawing a pentagram on the forehead of each participant.

The color correspondence for the water element is blue.

Air

The winter season is anchored by Aquarius, which is an air sign.

The air element is in the north and has projective energy.

The air elementals are the sylphs, which are tall, thin, and ethereal. They sometimes show themselves as winged, humanlike creatures.

Work with things that represent air whenever your magic is about intellect, learning, or music. The black-handled athame or the sword is the traditional tool, though in some traditions, it is the wand. Other items representing air are feathers, incense, chimes, wind instruments, smoke, censers, pens, fans, any blade, books, quills, sheet music, bells, and anything that stimulates thought. Birds, bats, dragonflies, and butterflies are of air.

Air represents learning, wisdom, music, the mind, analysis, communication, clear thinking, organization, strategy, and diplomacy. Air also represents your thoughts.

Some deities associated with air are Boreas, Greek god of the northern wind; Vayu, Hindu god of the wind; and Saraswati, Hindu goddess of knowledge, learning, and music. Some traditions associate Saraswati with water because of her origin as the goddess of a river.

The athame is the tool used to command space, stop negative projective energies directed at you, create sacred space, and consecrate other tools. Use the athame when you need to convey ideas, win an argument, take control of a situation, learn a new skill, play an instrument, pass a test, or another pursuit linked to air. The athame is purely a ritual tool, and you never use it to cut anything. It is traditional to keep a white-handled knife, a *boline*, to cut things with during ritual.

The color correspondence for the air element is yellow.

Elemental Correspondences Tables

These charts will cover the elemental correspondences that are most commonly used.

Element	Color	Cardinal Direction	Time of Day	Season
Earth	Green	East	Morning, sunrise	Spring
Fire	Red	South	Daytime, high noon	Summer
Water	Blue	West	Evening, sunset	Autumn
Air	Yellow	North	Nighttime, midnight	Winter

Element	Magical Tool	Characteristics	Elemental Being	Animals
Earth	Pentacle	Objects, grounding, steadfastness, nurturing, prosperity, fertility	Gnome	Mammals
Fire	Wand (athame or sword in some traditions)	Actions, ambition, passion, zeal, performance, fearlessness	Salamander	Reptiles
Water	Chalice	Emotions, empathy, compassion, healing	Undine	Fish, crustaceans, jellyfish
Air	Athame or sword (wand in some traditions)	Thoughts, intellect, musicality, analysis	Sylph	Birds, butterflies, dragonflies

Element	Tarot Suit	Card Suit	Crystals	Astrological Signs
Earth	Pentacles (also known as Discs or Coins)	Diamonds	Ruby, red jasper, obsidian, black tourmaline	Taurus, Virgo, Capricorn
Fire	Wands (also known as Rods, Staves, or Batons)	Clubs	Citrine, gold tiger's eye, pyrite, yellow topaz	Aries, Leo, Sagittarius

The Four Elements

Element	Tarot Suit	Card Suit	Crystals	Astrological Signs
Water	Cups	Hearts	Carnelian, orange calcite, copper, orange (red) aventurine, amber	Cancer, Scorpio, Pisces
Air	Swords	Spades	Rose quartz, emerald, bloodstone, kyanite (green)	Gemini, Libra, Aquarius

Element	Gender	Instruments	Substance	Items
Earth	Female, receptive	Drums	Salt	Wooden items, rocks, stones
Fire	Male, projective	Sistrums, rattles	Flame	Candles, oils, spirits, perfumes
Water	Female, receptive	String instruments (in some traditions)	Water or wine	Bowls, cups, divination tools, mermaids, seashells, pearls
Air	Male, projective	Wind instruments	Incense smoke	Incense, bells, fans, feathers

The Vast Meaning of the Elements

The correspondences listed in this chapter are the ones most commonly used today, but other color correspondences are also in use by witches.

At the basic level, all crystals are earth, and all musical instruments are air. However, it is more complicated and involved than that, as shown in these correspondences. The crystal correspondences, for example, are based on the chakra system of energy centers in the body. Again, these tables are by no means exhaustive.

Spell Using Only the Elements

Get dressed for the weather and then go outside. Find a place where you can be undisturbed for a few minutes. Now try to interact directly with the elements with simple spell work. Make sure to choose a specific intent before you begin.

Here are some examples of how you could do this:

- For a prosperity spell, turn to the east and say, "I prosper. I am always secure. I am stable and grounded. I am one with earth."

- For a spell of ambition, turn to the south and say, "I have passion and ambition, and I am fearless. I am one with fire."

- For a spell for emotions, turn to the west and say, "I have empathy, compassion, and finely tuned intuition. I am one with water."

- For an intellectual spell, turn to the north and say, "I have a strong intellect and musicianship. I have the ability to detach when needed. I am one with air."

If it suits your religious beliefs, you can end by looking up and stating a spiritual spell. For example: "I am the child of the Lady and the Lord. I am one with Spirit."

This ritual is quick and straightforward, and this is an excellent way to start every day. If the weather is not conducive to going outside, I do this when I shower in the morning.

Chapter 7

))))●●●(((

INCANTATIONS AND ENERGY

Expressing the goal that you wish to manifest precisely yet succinctly is vital for writing a successful spell. Verbose wordings, with lots of words that do not directly pertain to the intent, dilute the power of the spell. A spell using a powerful, unambiguous incantation is much more likely to succeed. This chapter will discuss how to write strong yet simple incantations.

Working with energy is another component of spell work. To execute your spells, you must also be adept at powering them with energy. This chapter will talk you through how to do that as well.

Chapter 7

Incantations

In spell work, it is traditional to write incantations that rhyme. If you find writing in verse challenging, try using a rhyming dictionary. Remember that you are not entering a poetry contest; your incantation can be simple and, from a poetry perspective, happily cringeworthy. If your incantation does not have a meter, that is fine. If it does, great.

If you decide not to write in verse, focus instead on making your incantation as clear and precise as possible. Remember to look at the ways your spell could backlash; be certain to plug those holes.

Also, remember that the Universe does not understand negatives well, so avoid using the words *no*, *don't*, and the like. State your incantation in the positive and in the present.

Below are some examples of short, rhyming incantations.

- Yesterday I fell, today I am well, for the greatest good of all, so mote it be.

- Advice to clients I tell, today twelve tarot readings I sell, for the greatest good of all, so mote it be.

- The test I pass, I ace this class, for the greatest good of all, so mote it be.

- (While lacing your running shoes): With magic my shoes I lace, I win the race, for the greatest good of all, so mote it be.

  - Note: this spell is on the boundary of what is ethical. Some would tell you that this is unethical because it works against the other competitors. I firmly believe that you have the right to further your own good if it does not directly work against a particular other person.

• I am fifteen pounds thinner, I am a great winner, I am healthy and whole, for the greatest good of all, so mote it be.

You get the idea. You can also write longer incantations if you wish, as long as what you write further specifies your intent. There is an example under the heading Acting in Accord of a non-rhyming, longer spell.

As you may have noticed, each of the example incantations ends with "For the greatest good of all, so mote it be." The first part of that phrase ensures that the spell will not accidentally negatively impact someone else. The second part is a traditional way to add power. A variation is "As I will, so mote it be."

Exercise: Rhyming Incantation

You will need

Pen and paper

For one of your goals, write an incantation that rhymes, if you can. If rhyming is challenging, simply restate your goal in poetic language that you feel suits you.

Exercise: House Clearing #1

You will need

Pen and paper

Salt

Cleansing herbs (e.g., bay leaf, lavender, and rosemary)

Write an incantation for a house clearing. Make sure that your wording clearly states that evil/unwanted spirits and negative energies are to leave and not come back.

Next, take salt and appropriate herbs from your kitchen spice cabinet. Walk around your living space deosil (sunwise) and sprinkle small amounts of your salt and herb mixture in each of the corners, all the while chanting your incantation.

Finally, sprinkle the mixture on each rug and in each area that has wall-to-wall carpet while chanting the incantation. Vacuum the rugs and carpets immediately so that the salt and spices do not grind into them.

On bare floors, you can leave the mixture in the corners for protection.

Raising Energy to Charge a Spell

For any spell to work, you need to create the desired outcome in the astral, then send energy to the physical plane at the time and place you desire the goal to be manifest. You may have heard the term *raising power* used. Power is the rate at which you send or receive energy. There are numerous ways to create the energy required for a spell to manifest; using several simultaneously is the most effective way to charge a spell. Here are some ways you can raise power:

- Let the object that holds the spell sit in the moonlight to charge it with energy. Then, you can use that energy when you cast the spell.

- Incantations have been used for millennia to raise energy. The more times an incantation is spoken, the more energy is raised. Likewise, if the incantation is sung as a chant rather than spoken, further energy is raised.

- The most important way to raise energy for spell work is to focus on the desired outcome, your emotions around that outcome, and the visualization. Remember that visualization is a critical step for creating the goal in the astral.

• Drawing down energy from the Universe and simultaneously drawing up energy from the earth will supercharge a spell. To do this, visualize white light coming from the Universe and entering through the top of your head, while red energy is coming from the center of the earth and entering through your feet. Visualize the white light traveling down toward your heart and the red light traveling up to meet the white light at your heart level. At this time, the energy may take on a green color or a rainbow hue. See the energy circle around your heart and then travel down through the arm, out through your projective hand, and into the object that holds your spell. See any remaining energy travel up your receptive arm and back to join with the energy circling your heart. As you get more adept at managing this energy flow, you can let the energy travel down both arms and into the object, then up through each arm, so that you have energy flowing both up and down in each arm.

When you send the spell out to do its work, push the energy to the time and place in the physical where you visualize the goal as being manifest.

Using Your Breath to Direct Magical Energy

Instead of using your hands to direct magical energy, you can use your breath. Using your breath is especially helpful to direct healing energy to scrapes, scratches, and bumps. My mother always did this when I got hurt as a child. It is comforting because you can feel the touch of the breath.

To use this technique, draw energy up from the earth and down from the Universe. Instead of having the energies meet at your heart, have them meet at your throat. Then blow out from your mouth, sending the energy into the target of your breath. Blowing energy works for any spell.

Using Your Eyes to Direct Magical Energy

For this method, draw up energy as before, but let the energy meet at your eyes this time. Then, send the energy out with your eyes to the object you are energizing.

As you gain experience, you can simultaneously send energy through your hands (either palms or fingers), your breath, and your eyes.

Energy for Astral Travel Spells

Astral travel spells need nothing other than your mind. They are quick yet powerful. You have already placed your goal on a timeline, so you know when it should manifest. Now, in your mind, walk the timeline to that point.

See yourself where you are when the goal manifests. Slip into your body at that future time. You are there. Focus on what it is like to be there. Listen and hear what you will hear, look around and see what you will see, and, most importantly, examine your reactions and *feel* what you will feel when your goal has manifested.

Notice what you are thinking. If you notice any smells or tastes, make a note of them as well. Return to your body in the here and now and say, "For the greatest good of all, so mote it be."

This way, you have created the manifest goal in a very profound way in the astral. You have sent a whole lot of power to the place and time of your goal manifesting. The Universe knows everything about the situation when the goal manifests and will adjust for it to be so.

To Document or Not to Document

When casting a spell, should you write down what you did? Opinions vary widely on this. Some say, "Absolutely not. Documenting a spell would ruin the magic." These are the "set it and forget it" witches. The argument is that if you document a spell, you will keep going back to look at it before it has had time to come to fruition, and you will send doubt into the Universe. For your spell to work, you must have absolute trust that it will work. If you doubt it, doubt is what you create in the Universe. When the Universe mirrors doubt, chances are that the Universe will not manifest what you aimed for. Why should it? It hears that there is uncertainty about whether this is to be manifest. Therefore, the argument goes that after you cast your spell, you should actively forget it so that you cannot doubt it.

On the other hand, there is good reason to document what you did. For a Thoughtform, which can hang around indefinitely, you want to be able to go back and look up what you programmed it to do! (We will talk more about Thoughtforms in chapter 12.)

When you have performed a very successful spell, you probably will want to pattern future spells on it, so having documentation that you can reference would be helpful. And, for a spell that was not successful, after the time for the goal to manifest has passed, you might want to go back and analyze what went wrong. You might ask yourself:

- Did I get the correct correspondences?

- Did I work with an appropriate deity?

- Was my timeline appropriate and reasonable?

- Did I write down and execute the steps to Act in Accord?

It is difficult to do this analysis if you do not have all the details written down.

There is, of course, a longstanding tradition of documenting spells. A grimoire is a book of spells and incantations. The Atharva Veda, part of one of the oldest books in the world, is full of spells, and so is the *Key of Solomon*. And many witches have spells written in their Book of Shadows, especially if they do not keep a separate grimoire for spells.

I document spells that are complex and let the quickie ones go without documentation. Having complex spells written down saves me time if I want to do the spell again, once I have the same need. As an example, I once learned a spell for selling property from Gavin Bone. I understood how it worked, and I wrote it down. I have successfully used it repeatedly, and I did not have to sit down and spend any time creating a new spell—I just had to look it up and cast it.

As you can tell, I lean heavily in the direction of documenting. I have enough self-control not to go around worrying about a spell I have cast, nor do I second-guess myself while it is in flight. If this is something you might find challenging, there are some work-arounds. You can use paper clips to hold pages closed if you documented your spells in a physical book. If you documented them digitally, keep each spell that is in flight in a separate file until the spell has succeeded or timed out.

Whether or not you choose to document your spells, you should always document the steps for Acting in Accord. Even if there are only a few steps and they seem simple, write them down. This way, you have a way to measure your progress. You will also need the steps documented if you have to tweak the spell and cast it again later.

Many practitioners keep beautiful books in which to document their spells; this was especially common in the past. You can still find gorgeous handmade books or binders in marketplaces. But you can just as easily write your spells in a regular notebook or binder, or keep them in a digital notebook.

A binder makes it easy to organize the spells by type or by date, and binders also make it easy to add notes later regarding the success or failure of the working. With that being said, digital spell books are becoming more and more common. If you keep your collection of spells in cloud storage, digital spell books have the great benefit of accessibility from anywhere you have internet access. Your collection is also safe from being lost or stolen that way. Physical books that contain spells can be attractive to unethical magic practitioners, though it usually does not work out well for the thief. If you do use a physical book, make sure to protect it with a spell to prevent theft or loss.

Exercise: Spell Book

As I have pointed out before, I find it very useful to document spells, other than the very simplest ones. If you elect not to document your spells, you can skip this exercise, or you can use it to document the steps for Acting in Accord, which you always need to write down.

I have a three-ring binder that I use for spells and other important magical documentation. My first ring binder for this purpose had plastic pockets on the front and back covers, and I put paper sheets decorated with protective symbols in them. Now I have a binder with leather covers that has an encircled pentagram embossed on it. At one point in the past, I used a pretty notebook with an owl embossed on the cover. You can use any notebook or binder that you feel drawn to. Decorate it with your own drawings, photographs, printouts from the internet, or scrapbooking materials. I keep my most important and sacred writings in a small leather-bound notebook that was given to me by my teachers. I have put several protection spells on that book.

Increasingly, I have been using a digital notebook, as I travel a lot and don't carry my binder with me. Once I've returned home, I usually transcribe what is in my digital notebook onto a page in my binder. Sometimes I print out something from my digital notebook and glue it onto a page in my binder.

You will need
A notebook or ring binder, or a digital notebook

Start a physical or digital spell book. This is where you will document the spells you perform.

If you've chosen a physical book, decorate it to your liking. If it is digital, find appropriate symbols/pictures and copy them into the first page of the book. Put a protection spell on the book.

Chapter 8

))))●●●((((

PREPARING FOR MAGIC

B eing prepared is essential for magic, just as it is for most mundane undertakings. One of the most important things you can prepare is the space you will do magic in. You need to decide what kind of energy you want that space to have. In some circumstances, I suggest that you work with a magical circle, but in other circumstances, there is no need. We will discuss how to create a magical circle later in this chapter.

Before doing magic, you also need to prepare yourself. Both your body and mind need to be energetically ready to do the work. We will discuss that kind of preparation in this chapter as well.

Performing Spells with or without a Circle

You can perform all of your spells in a Wiccan circle if you choose to. We will discuss how to set up a circle in this chapter. But if you feel that a circle is not necessary for you, then do without it. I think that magic is safer and more powerful when performed in a circle. The circle holds the energy you are raising inside it until you are ready to send it through the circle wall; no power can trickle out by mistake while you are working the spell.

As a Wiccan High Priestess, I tend to do magic work inside a circle. Having said that, spells can certainly be done impromptu and without a circle. For example, I once attended a concert where one of the performing choirs was very mediocre. I thought to myself (with strong emotion), *The audience deserves so much better than this. I can get a group together and do much, much better than this!* I visualized myself and a group of singers in the place of the current choir, in that exact venue and at that yearly event. I barely realized that I had cast a spell, but of course, I had. A year or two later (and for several years afterward), I ended up having a group perform at the event. The group received great acclaim, and one year a local TV station even featured the group on the news. The spell worked because of my heartfelt belief that the audience deserved a better, more authentic performance.

Setting Up a Magical Circle

The four elements used in magic are earth, fire, water, and air. (Refer back to chapter 6 for more about the elements.) Suffice it to say that the energies of all four elements need to be present for a goal to manifest on the physical plane. The most effective and safe way of doing this in my mind is in a circle, also called a magical circle. The circle contains the power raised by the spell work until the practitioner deliberately releases it into the Universe. The circle also contains the elemental energies within it.

A magical practitioner casts a protective circle using an incantation. Then, in the next step, they call the elemental energies into the circle. Casting a circle can be as simple as walking around in a circular shape, calling up energy with an incantation, and visualizing that energy as a blue electric sphere surrounding you. While some magical traditions have a standard, specified incantation for circle casting, others write a new incantation for each circle. Sometimes practitioners recite a chant written for that purpose. For spell-casting purposes, you may use something simple like:

"O Circle, I conjure thee to let in all love and keep out all evil, to contain the magical power until I release it, and to keep the elemental energies within."

If you decide to write your own incantation, the key pieces to include are allowing the positive, keeping out the negative / evil, and containing the magic until you are ready to release it. If you are working with religious magic, you would also add, "I bless and consecrate thee in the names of [Goddess] and [God]." This sentence is from the standard British Traditional Wicca circle cast.

After casting your circle through your incantation, you call in the elements. The cardinal direction placement of the elements is earth in the east, fire in the south, water in the west, and air in the north. (I practice with air in the north and earth in the east to be consistent with the astrological directions of the elements.) In order for the elemental energies to come into the physical plane, you need to have a representation of each of the elements present in the circle. You can use a bowl of dirt or salt for earth, a lit candle for fire, a bowl of water for water, and lit incense for air (where the smoke represents air). Then draw an invoking pentagram and encircle it in each of the four cardinal directions while saying an incantation for each quarter. (More about invoking and banishing pentagrams can be found in chapter 4.) As you walk the circle in each cardinal direction, visualize the realm of the corresponding element through the pentagon in the middle of the pentacle and then visualize that elemental energy entering and spinning around the perimeter of the circle.

If that paragraph was all gibberish to you, call in the elemental energies as follows:

1. Stand near the perimeter of your circle, in the east and facing the east, and state: "Guardians of the elementals of the east, I invite you to bring in the earth elemental energy." The energy will arrive! Visualize green energy spinning around the perimeter of the circle.

2. Do the same in the south for fire, and visualize red energy spinning around the circle.

3. In the west, call in water and visualize blue energy spinning around the circle.

4. Finally, in the north, call in air and visualize yellow energy spinning around the circle.

5. Once you have called in all four elemental energies, visualize them melding into one sparkling, electric-blue energy around the circle.

Note that you do not have to go through all the steps of casting a circle if you are doing something like a little spell to add love to the food you're preparing; just do your magic. Similarly, if you are drawing a banishing pentagram and throwing it at some negative energy coming at you, just do it. When and whether to use a circle is situational. Use your judgment!

If you are working with religious magic, you can invite the deity into the circle to be with you. Remember to thank them later.

Then, face north and describe the deity by name and in at least two other ways so that they know that you are calling them and not another deity or entity. For example:

"Lovely Freya, thou glorious bringer of love and of riches, daughter of Njord and sister of Frey; I invite thee to attend this circle and ask thee to lend thy magical power to my working."

If you want to use this example as a guideline for your own invocation but the language feels stilted to you, you can modify the sentence. You can do this by changing "thou" to "you," "thee" to "you," and "thy" to "your."

Now that your circle is cast and all the energy has been called in, it is time to do your spell! When you cast your spell—at the moment when you say, "So mote it be"—visualize the power that you have raised bursting forth into the Universe.

Then it is time to wrap things up. If you invited a deity or deities, thank them while facing north. For example:

"Lovely Freja, I thank you for attending this circle, and ere you depart to your pleasant and lovely realm, I bid you hail and farewell."

The wording above is partly based on the text for the closing quarter calls in British Traditional Wicca. Again, you can modify it to your liking.

Then return to the east and thank the guardians. "Guardians of the elementals of the east, I thank you for bringing the earth elemental energies, and I bid you farewell." Then bow. Repeat this for each element in the appropriate direction.

Some books instruct you to move widdershins (countersunwise) when opening a circle back up at the end of a ritual or spell-casting session, but I always move deosil (sunwise) in the circle, even when dismissing the quarters. This is because this is the way that the sun and the moon both travel, whether they are rising (starting) or setting (ending).

✦ ✦ ✦

Now that we have discussed the basics of casting a circle, think about whether or not you want to cast a circle before performing spell work. If you want to work in a circle, decide whether you plan to use the incantations I provided or whether you would prefer to write your own. If you are going to use the ones presented here, learn them by heart now. You do not want to be reading out of a book when you need to focus on the energy work that you are doing. If you want to write your own incantations, try your hand at it now. Write a generic circle cast and generic quarter calls. Make them generic in the sense that they are not specific to a particular goal. This way, you will be prepared when it is time to do spell work.

Preparing Yourself for Magic

When you do magic, you create the outcome in the astral plane and channel energy from the Universe to a specific time and place or for a specific purpose. You are the conduit, and as such, your body and your mind should both be prepared.

For your body to be prepared to do a simple spell at any time of the day, think of every shower you take as an opportunity to cleanse yourself energetically as well as physically. As the water cleans your body, visualize the water also washing off any negative energy that might have found its way onto you. Envision yourself as energetically clean and whole. This routine will adequately prepare you for simple spells such as putting love into your food.

Further Preparation

For a complex spell that you have put a lot of time and effort into designing, or for a spell that carries great significance for you, you should further prepare your body and mind right before casting the spell.

If you have a bathtub, taking a ritual bath is an excellent way to prepare. Before you step into the bath, take a shower and watch as anything negative rinses off you. Ground yourself by letting any excess energy flow into Mother Earth and draw up fresh energy from Her.

Light purifying incense or herbs such as frankincense, myrrh, bay leaves, cedar, thyme, basil, cloves, or dragon's blood. Then start to fill the tub with water and add cleansing herbs or oils to it. If you choose to add essential oils, make sure you have a dropper and a carrier oil such as almond oil, olive oil, apricot kernel oil, or jojoba oil. Using your dropper, mix ten drops of essential oil with one tablespoon of a carrier oil, then add this mixture to the bathwater. Rosemary essential oil is a good choice for cleansing, as are frankincense oil or myrrh oil. Caution: adding oils to your bath before stepping in could make the tub slippery. Alternatively, you could add some table salt to the bath for purification. Use a salt that is not iodized if you can.

Light candles in colors that support your goal (more about color correspondences in chapter 5). Then step in and soak in the bath. Focus inward and on the spell work that you are about to do. Shut out the mundane world from your mind and prepare for magic.

When you get out of the bath, extinguish any lit flames and then dress in all clean clothes. If you have special robes or other garments set aside for magic, this is the time to don them. Keeping a set of special or unique clothes for magic helps you step into your power as you put them on. You can actually feel the energy shift around you! Robes and cloaks are popular choices, but anything you will wear only during magical workings is fine. Note that robes and cloaks with very wide sleeves look and feel very magical but can be hazardous around burning candles.

Many people find it helpful to have a special place to do magic, a special surface reserved for performing spells. It can be as simple as a cutting board or a tray that you put away after each magical use and do not use for any mundane purposes. The object will build magical power in itself by being used repeatedly. Having an object that you can bring out also helps you get in the right mindset for magic and directs the right amount of focus on the working at hand.

It is also helpful to set the stage before a working. Lighting candles and incense can set the mood and help you focus. You can choose a magically supporting fragrance to layer the magic for a specific goal. Alternatively, you could always use the same scent of incense during spell work, which will help shift your mindset to magic when lit. Dragon's blood is appropriate, as is a blend of juniper, cedar, and sandalwood. The latter three can be bought individually as incense sticks or cones and burned simultaneously, or you could use essential oils. If you use essential oils, fill an aromatherapy oil burner with water and add two to three drops of each oil into the water.

Finally, just before starting your spell work, take a moment to gather yourself, ground, and center. Close your eyes and take a deep breath. Feel how you are connected to the earth. Envision roots growing from your feet down into the earth, and feel all excess energy draining down through these roots. Notice how this makes you feel balanced, steady, and calm. Find stillness within yourself. Then focus on a point between your navel and solar plexus and center within yourself for a moment. When you feel ready, visualize pulling up your roots but don't lose the connection you've made with the earth. Keep the same calmness and stillness within. Open your eyes. Now you are prepared to do magic.

Part Three

))))●●●◑●((((

TYPES ⊙F SPELLS

Chapter 9

)))◗●◖(((

THE MOST COMMON SPELLS

There exist a nearly infinite number of types of spells. For this chapter, I have selected the types of spells that are the most common. While choosing spells, I also made sure that the way they work is easy to understand. Candle magic, various types of cord magic, mirror magic, jar spells, and paper spells are all in the repertoire of nearly every practitioner. This chapter also has some other types of spells that I have found highly useful over the years and that you may wish to include in your magical toolbox.

Candle Magic

For basic candle magic spells,

You will need

A candle, preferably small

Matches or a lighter

A safe surface to burn a candle on

Oil(s) to anoint the candle with

Something to inscribe words and symbols on the candle
(optional)

Body or face paint crayons (optional)

Napkin or tissue (required if using paint)

Pin (optional, useful for large candles)

Candle spells can be as simple as selecting a candle of the color that represents the goal and lighting it while visualizing the goal as manifest, then burning it fully down. In order for the spell to be completely released to the Universe, the entire candle should burn down until it self-extinguishes. A partially released spell can cause havoc and misfire badly.

Ensure that the candle holder you choose can tolerate the resulting heat and that it is on a surface that will not be destroyed or catch on fire. Because you want the candle to burn down entirely, it is advisable to choose smaller candles, sometimes called spell candles. For more modest goals, you can use birthday candles. If you don't have an appropriately sized candle holder, a wad of aluminum foil that is large enough to keep the candle stable works very well.

Light the candle with intent while visualizing your goal as already manifested. Say your incantation while purposefully imbuing the candle with your intent and emotion, then let the candle burn fully. Examples of such simple candle spells are:

- Burn a green candle for prosperity (earth correspondence).

- Burn a red candle to perform well in a sporting event (fire correspondence).

- Burn a blue candle to send healing (water correspondence).

- Burn a yellow candle to perform well on an academic test (air correspondence).

- Burn a pink candle to draw love to you (heart chakra correspondence).

- Burn a yellow candle for the strength to put your foot down about an issue you are facing (solar plexus chakra correspondence) and a blue candle to be able to communicate your new boundary in a clear, firm, and diplomatic fashion (throat chakra correspondence).

For more complex or more significant goals, ask yourself the "Check the Ecosystem" questions from chapter 2. If you are ready, move on to find the place on the timeline when your goal will manifest, as described earlier. Next, document the steps you need to take to Act in Accord.

More complex candle spells involve carving appropriate words and symbols on the candle. Such spells typically require at least a spell-size candle. The carving can be rubbed with a body or face-painting crayon of an appropriate color for extra magical layering. Regular crayons tend to be too hard to work well. Instead, rub face paint all over the carving, then wipe the excess off with a paper napkin or toilet paper. The color will remain in the grooves of the carving.

Spell candles are available in some metaphysical shops and online. Tools for carving can usually be found either in your tool chest or in a hobby store. In a brick-and-mortar hobby store, they are found in the aisle where clay is kept.

If you have only large candles on hand, an alternative to burning the entire candle is to stick a pin into the candle a bit below the top. Then make only the part above the pin the focus of the spell and burn the candle until the pin drops. In this situation, you can then snuff the candle out. Since only the part above the pin was infused with the magic of your spell, you can use the same candle again for a different spell. One note: you need to use a somewhat soft candle for the pin to penetrate enough to stay put.

Layering the candle spell with appropriate essential oils increases its power. Oil correspondences are a broad field of study and were only touched on in chapter 5. A simple way to work with anointing oils for candle spells is to have at least one banishing oil and one manifesting oil. For a banishing, start anointing the candle on its ends and pull the oil toward the middle. This pulls what you are banishing out of the Universe and burns it. For manifesting, start the oil at the middle of the candle and pull it out toward the ends. Doing this sends what you are manifesting to the Universe. An alternative way of anointing a candle is to start the oil at the bottom and anoint upward if your spell is to manifest something new. Start the oil at the top and pull downward if your spell is to banish something from your life. If you anoint a carved candle, do not put oil where the colored inscriptions are, as this will cause the coloring to bleed.

If you are using herbs with your candle magic, make sure the herbs are crushed and then roll the bottom of the candle in them. Ensure that you have sufficiently large fireproof protection under the candle, just in case any glowing flakes of herbs fall off while you are burning the candle.

Before doing candle magic, visualize your goal as manifest in the astral plane in order to create it on that plane. Then charge the candle with energy and light it while visualizing the place and time where the goal needs to manifest in the physical plane. The candle will continue to send the magical energy as it burns. When the candle has burned down, take your first step to Act in Accord.

Send Healing Using Candle Magic

YOU WILL NEED

A candle in an appropriate color for healing (e.g., blue)

Oil for anointing the candle

Matches or a lighter

A place where the candle can safely burn down completely

Ask someone who is not feeling well due to a minor ailment or someone who is sad if you may send them healing. When a friend agrees, pick a candle of an appropriate color. I recommend blue. Then choose an essential oil to anoint the candle, doing so as described in this chapter. (Olive oil works if you do not have an appropriate oil at home.)

Once you've finished anointing the candle, set it somewhere safe and light it. While lighting the candle, visualize healing energy coming up from the earth through your feet and traveling upward. Also visualize healing energy coming down from the Universe through the top of your head and traveling downward. See the energies meet at your heart and go through your arms.

Hold your open palms toward the lit candle and visualize the healing energy going to the candle and from the candle to your friend. Visualize your friend healthy and happy.

Because you have imbued the entire candle with the spell, let the candle burn all the way down.

Cord Magic

Cord magic works on the principle of locking the intent of a spell into a cord or knot. In this section, you will learn several different types of cord magic.

The Witch's Ladder

A witch's ladder is a cord where you tie your goal into nine knots, each knot with the same intent. Unlike most spells, you can break up this work over time by tying one knot at a time. If you do so, make sure that you have coherence in the timing, e.g., every day at the same time, every other day at the same time, every Diana's Bow, etc. Such consistency helps build power.

Like you would for candle magic, start by asking yourself the "Check the Ecosystem" questions in chapter 2. If you feel ready to proceed, choose the right time for the goal to manifest, then document the steps to Act in Accord.

To create a basic witch's ladder, it is traditional to use a cord that is a multiple of nine inches, three feet, or nine feet long. Select a cord color that supports your goal. You can also braid together three colors that support your goal to create the cord.

You might want to light a tea candle and let the wax melt, then dip the ends of the cord(s) in the wax, away from the flame or with the flame extinguished. This seals the ends of the cord with candle wax so they do not fray.

Witch's Ladder

You will need

A three-foot cord

Pen

Book of Shadows, grimoire, or magical notebook for
documentation

Items that support your goal, which will be tied into the ladder
(optional)

Write down one of your goals. You are going to be using that
goal to create a witch's ladder.

Hold the top of the cord in your nondominant hand. With
your dominant hand, draw a banishing pentagram over the cord to
cleanse it. Visualize any darkness in the cord sinking to the ground
and into the earth, where it will be transmuted.

Consecrate the cord by drawing an invoking pentagram over it
while you visualize red energy coming from the ground and rising
up through your feet, up through your legs, and into your torso.
Notice how the red energy picks up orange tones several inches
below the navel. Near the solar plexus, some of the energy turns
yellow, and green is added to the mix near your heart. Also, visualize violet and white sparkling energy coming from the Universe
to the top of your head and traveling downward. At the forehead,
some energy takes on shades of purple and indigo; at your throat,
some energy picks up blue tones; and at your heart, some green
is added. When the two energy streams meet at your heart, they
create a fountain of rainbow, sparkling energy. Next, visualize
the rainbow sparkles going down your left arm and out through
your left hand, through the cord, and back into your right hand,
up through your right arm, and back to the heart. Finally, visualize

the energy moving in this circle for about a minute; see the cord glowing and sparkling with the rainbow energies. Your cord is now cleansed and consecrated.

Charge the cord with each of the elements. If you are in a circle, bring the cord to your altar. Rub some cornmeal or soil on it, quickly bring it through the south quarter candle flame, dip it in the water, and wave it through incense smoke. Then go deosil (sunwise) to the east quarter (cardinal direction) and state, "I charge thee [or you] with the element of earth." Next, go to the south and charge the cord with the element of fire by using this same statement, modifying the element name. Then go to the west to charge with water and to the north to charge with air. Your cord is ready to receive its programming.

The traditional way of programming the cord is by tying nine knots in it. You can tie supporting items into the cord or just tie knots. It is customary to tie feathers into the knots, but you can choose other items that support your goal through correspondence. If you'd rather not include anything in your knots, that is fine too.

Now it is time to chant and tie the knots. Visualize the goal as already manifested as you chant and tie the knots, using this traditional pattern and chant:

))))●●●(((

By knot of ONE, the spell's begun	1--------
By knot of TWO, it cometh true	1-------2
By knot of THREE, so mote it be	1---3---2
By knot of FOUR, the power I store	1-4-3---2
By knot of FIVE, the spell's alive	1-4-3-5-2
By knot of SIX, this spell I fix	164-3-5-2

By knot of SEVEN, events I will leaven   164-3-572

By knot of EIGHT, my will be Fate   16483-572

By knot of NINE, what is done is mine   164839572

))))●●●((((

Bury the witch's ladder in the earth for manifestation. As soon as you have buried the cord, take your first step to Act in Accord. Then, as the cord decays, the intent will be sent to the Universe.

An alternative to burying the cord is to open up the knots, one at a time, in the same order that you tied them, using the same incantation to release the power of each knot. If, by chance, your cord is synthetic, this is the method you need to use. Synthetic cords will not decay if you bury them, at least not in a reasonable time frame. Discard the cord once you have untied the knots.

Exercise: Witch's Ladder Variation

This exercise is almost exactly the same as the previous one, except for this variation, you should first write down your goal, then add eight details or refinements of it. An example of this would be:

1. I own a house that I can live in.

2. My house is in a safe area.

3. My house is conveniently located by where I work, has access to nature trails, and has nearby grocery shopping.

4. My house has at least two bedrooms.

5. My house has at least one-and-a-half bathrooms.

6. My house has a garden where I can grow vegetables, herbs, fruits, and berries.

7. My house has a two-car garage.

8. My house has an area set aside for magical workings.

9. My house has a kitchen with a stove that has at least one oven, at least four burners, and a convection feature, and the kitchen also has a dishwasher, refrigerator, and freezer.

Proceed with the steps of the previous witch's ladder exercise, but when you tie the knots, visualize each independent aspect of your goal as you tie the corresponding numbered knot. Visualize one aspect per knot.

Cord Magic to Protect Against Theft

You will need

Nine-inch piece of string or thin yarn

Take a nine-inch piece of string or thin yarn. Stand in front of the item that you want to protect. Visualize a protective ring around the object, then visualize that ring going into the string or yarn as you tie a knot in it. Lay the string next to the object and visualize the protective ring coming from the knot.

This spell relies on the Law of Similarity. By tying the knot, you are tying the item to where it is located.

State, "As I tie this knot, I tie protection to this item from theft or loss, for the greatest good of all, so mote it be."

Your item is safe. Remember to untie the knot before you want to move or use the item.

Simple Braided Spell

You will need

Three cords, either nine-inch cords or cords that are three feet or nine feet long

Pen

Book of Shadows, grimoire, or magical notebook for
documentation

In this spell, you put your goal into the entire cord. For quick,
simple spells, three thin, nine-inch cords will work well. For more
serious work, use three three-foot cords or three nine-foot cords.
Working with three nine-foot cords will take a significant amount
of time to braid (likely an hour to two hours, depending on how
fast you braid) and will therefore have more potent magic.

To start with, prepare the cords like you would for a traditional
witch's ladder. Next, cleanse the three strands and seal the edges in
wax. Write a short incantation connected to your goal, preferably
both with rhyme and meter. You will be saying this many times
over.

Begin to braid the three cords together. Visualize your goal as
already manifest, braiding as you say the incantation repeatedly.
Doing this places the goal firmly in the cord. When you come
to the end, tie the three ends together so that the braid will not
unravel. Now you can wear the braid, bury it outside, or hide it in
a tree.

Mirror Magic

A magical mirror can be either a highly polished obsidian (also
called a scrying mirror because of its common usage) or a regular
mirror with a frame. In either case, when you first get your magical mirror, you need to cleanse it. Cleansing can be done by burying the mirror temporarily in dirt, immersing it in running water,
cleaning it with lemon, dipping it in salt water and then rinsing it,

or waving it in incense smoke. You can also surround the mirror with kyanite and citrine crystals for cleansing.

If you are using a regular mirror with a frame, it is customary to decorate the frame with magical symbols of your choice. For example, choose a mirror with a white frame and decorate it with gold or silver paint, or choose a mirror with a dark frame and decorate it with gold, silver, or white paint.

Some magical mirrors are concave. Unfortunately, these can be hard to find, and high-quality ones can be expensive.

Cleansing with a Magical Mirror

Once your magical mirror has been cleansed, it can be used to cleanse other things. Place the object that you wish to cleanse on the mirror. The mirror image of the object will absorb any gunk in the object. When you remove the object from the mirror, the mirror image disappears and takes the undesirable energies with it. A magical mirror will typically not need to be cleansed after being used like this, as all the nastiness has disappeared.

Mirror Spell for Confidence

YOU WILL NEED

A magical mirror

Incantation

Pen

Book of Shadows, grimoire, or magical notebook for
    documentation

Standing up, hold your magical mirror in front of your face. Straighten your back, keep your shoulders down, and lift your chin just a tiny bit.

Let your eyes unfocus and visualize yourself in the mirror as the person you want to be: strong, confident, and with the looks you desire. State an appropriate incantation, e.g., "I am powerful, I am fearless, I am poised" as you do so.

Say the incantation three times, a little louder each time. After the third time, quickly lower the mirror and sit down. Relax.

Mirror Spell for Self-Love

YOU WILL NEED

A magical mirror

Two candles

Matches or a lighter

A table to sit at

Pen

Paper

Sit down at a table where you have placed a pair of candles a few feet away from you. One candle should be a little to your left and one a little to your right.

On a piece of paper, write down how you want to feel about yourself, but address yourself in the second person, e.g., "I love you," "I am happy with you," "I really like you," and other similar self-love statements.

Turn off the lights or dim them. Light the two candles.

Hold up your magical mirror and take a good look at yourself. Smile at yourself—*really* smile. Then say the statements that you wrote down on the paper to yourself in the mirror. Keep smiling.

It is a good idea to remember to smile at yourself every time you see yourself in a mundane mirror as well.

Chapter 9

Jar Spells

A jar spell is any spell that is contained in a jar. You may have heard of a witch's bottle; it is a type of jar spell.

To do a jar spell, as usual, check the soundness of what you are manifesting. If you decide to manifest something, define the time and the steps needed to Act in Accord. Then select a small- to medium-sized jar. A toddler food jar is usually about the right size. If you plan to add many items to your jar spell, choose a jam jar. Clean the jar physically, then cleanse it energetically by letting it sit in moonlight or rain overnight.

Once the empty jar has been cleansed, place it on your altar with the intent that it will manifest your goal. Putting an empty jar on your altar will charge it with magical energy. If you are not working with an altar, set the jar out in moonlight again with the intent to charge it.

The next step is to add magical items to the jar. While visualizing your goal as manifest, fill the jar with items that correspond to the goal you wish to manifest. You may fill the jar with crystals, pictures of your goal, or colored items that correspond with your goal. You can add drops of an essential oil that supports your goal, or create an infusion (tea) or tincture (herbs soaked in alcohol) using herbs that support your goal and add that to the jar.

Once you have added all your items, hide the jar where it will never be found. This usually entails digging a relatively deep hole and burying it. If the jar breaks or is found, the spell is broken. If you are doing a protection jar for a home being built, for example, you may want to place the jar in between wall studs so that it is built into the home's framework.

Witch's Bottle

YOU WILL NEED

A glass jar with a lid

A place to hide the jar

Something from the person to be protected (e.g., hair or nail clippings or urine)

Nails and pins

Prewritten protection incantation

Pen

Book of Shadows, grimoire, or magical notebook for documentation

Rosemary or frankincense essential oil (optional)

A witch's bottle is usually created to protect someone against spells cast against them. It contains something to tie the bottle to the person, typically their urine or hair, and items of protection like nails and pins, which impale spells sent toward the person for whom the bottle was made. You can also add something that purifies, e.g., rosemary or frankincense oil, to purge and annihilate evil that has been impaled in the bottle.

Make sure to state an incantation of protection as you fill the jar.

Again, a witch's bottle must be hidden. If the jar breaks or is found, the protection ends. Like any jar spell, the most common way of ensuring that a witch's bottle will not be found is to bury it underground.

Honey Jar Spell

YOU WILL NEED

A glass jar with a lid

A place to bury the jar

Paper or birch bark to write on

Pen

Book of Shadows, grimoire, or magical notebook for
documentation

A sweetener (e.g., honey, syrup, or sugar water)

Beeswax

Prewritten love incantation (optional)

Symbols of sweetness (optional)

A honey jar spell is used when you need to become a better, sweeter, more loving, more lovable person. A couple can also use it to strengthen their love for each other. It is a beautiful part of a handfasting or wedding. Everyone attending can help charge the jar for the couple, or, if the couple prefers, they can choose to be the only ones adding energy to the jar. If the couple likes more privacy, they can create a honey jar alone before or after the ceremony.

To create a honey jar, you will need a jar with a lid, something to write on, and a sweetener. As the name suggests, honey is traditional, but any natural sweetener will do the trick. The sweetener is the ingredient that will sweeten a person or their feelings.

As with any jar spell, start by physically cleaning the jar, energetically cleansing it, and charging it. When you are ready to create the spell, write your name if the spell is for you alone. If the spell is for you and your lover, write both of your names. Some people like to write the names ninety degrees across each other. Whichever way you do it, make it as pretty as you can. You want it SWEET! Add hearts, roses, and any other symbols that represent the type of sweetness you are seeking to manifest with the spell. Be sure to focus on your intent as you decorate. Then place the paper inside the jar. If you want, you can also put real roses and other objects of sweetness in the jar.

Now you are ready to add the sweetener. You can say an incantation while you add the sweetener to layer the magic. Pour the sweetener into the jar while visualizing your goal, and then put the lid on the jar.

You may add wax around the seal if you are so inclined. To do this, carefully melt beeswax on slow heat and dip the top of the jar in the wax. Let it cool. Inscribe a heart or other appropriate symbol in the wax.

Bury the jar.

Ending Love Jar

YOU WILL NEED

A glass jar with a lid

A place to bury the jar

Paper

Pen

A bitter liquid (e.g., overly strong tea or burned coffee)

Vinegar

Prewritten incantation

Book of Shadows, grimoire, or magical notebook for
    documentation

If someone is overly enthusiastic about pursuing you and you are not interested, you have the right to protect yourself from emotional harm and potential danger. While this spell interferes with the free will of another person, I consider it one of the situational ethics situations discussed in chapter 2. Here, your emotional and physical safety is what is most important.

For this spell, find a clean and cleansed jar with a lid. Then write your name and the person's name on a piece of paper. Draw a circle around the names and draw a slash through it, separating your name from theirs. Above the paper, draw a banishing pentagram with your hand, then place the paper in the jar.

Make a bitter mixture of much-too-strong tea, burned coffee, or another bitter liquid that you have on hand. Add vinegar to this to sour it. This type of spell is the complete opposite of a honey jar.

Say an incantation that sets forth that the person no longer pursues you, for the greatest good of all.

Finally, bury the jar.

Paper Spells

A paper spell is any spell where either the totality or a significant part of the working consists of words or images on a piece of paper. These are simple to create and quick to perform. Consequently, they are in widespread use. They are very effective if done right.

Start, as usual, by ensuring that your goal is sound, writing your Acting in Accord list, and establishing the timeline for the spell to work.

Then write down an incantation for your goal, preferably but not necessarily in rhymed format. Make sure the incantation is in the positive and in the present tense, as if it already is true. Alternatively, draw images of your goal already being manifest or glue pictures onto the paper. Images can come from photographs, the internet, magazines, or any other source; the only important aspect is that they depict your goal as already being manifest. Next, add symbols and colors that, via correspondence, support your goal.

To cast the spell, intently visualize the goal as already being manifest, and use one of the following methods to send the goal to the Universe:

- Bury the paper in the ground, where Mother Earth will work with you to manifest your goal. This is especially powerful for goals that deal with prosperity, abundance, and manifesting wealth. It is also highly effective for seeking grounding. Blessings for the beginning of projects also work well when buried.

- Burn the paper in a fire in a brazier, fire ring, or fireplace. This is very powerful for banishings. It also works well for manifestations, as the smoke carries the intent to the Universe. This method also works exceptionally well for fire-related goals, e.g., increased ambition, drive, passion, performance, physical energy, and the like.

- Place the paper in a lake, the ocean, a stream, or any body of water. This water element method is especially effective if you are trying to draw love to you, if you are looking to become more loving or empathetic, or if your spell is for physical or emotional healing. Spells for mental health belong here. Goals that deal with improving magical skills also belong here. Make sure that you use paper that will break down quickly and entirely.

- Go to a high point, then let the wind take the paper. This air-element method is best for goals relating to intellectual capacity, musical endeavors, book writing, study skills and study habits, academic success, etc. Again, make sure that your paper is fully biodegradable and will disappear quickly. You do not want to litter, nor do you want anyone to lay eyes on your spell.

After you've released your paper spell, take the first step on your Acting in Accord plan to enable the magic to work.

In all cases, please make certain that you choose papers and ink that are nontoxic and biodegradable. Please do not litter! If you have access to birch bark instead of paper, that is an outstanding choice for all four approaches.

Also, remember that the water approach—and especially the air approach—may expose your goals to strangers. This is highly undesirable, as it may negate your magic. If you use one of those two approaches, you may wish to write your goals in a hard-to-decipher script or state your goal entirely in symbols, with no text.

Paper Spell

YOU WILL NEED

Pen

Paper or birch bark

Book of Shadows, grimoire, or magical notebook for
    documentation

For one of your goals, write a quick, uncomplicated spell on paper or birch bark. Cast your paper spell in one of the four ways described, depending on which element it is most connected to.

Paper Spell for Successful Vending at an Event
You will need

Paper

Pen

Marjoram

Nutmeg

Cumin

A coin, preferably the largest denomination in the currency used wherever the event is held

Knowledge of how to draw the symbol for the planet Mercury

Knowledge of how to draw the symbol for the zodiac sign Taurus

An envelope

A place to burn or bury the envelope

This spell is an example of a paper spell that enhances the probability that you will sell well as a vendor at an event, and it also ensures that none of your items will be stolen. You may wish to take a ritual bath before starting.

Select the paper you are going to use. If you have parchment, you may want to use that. Also, get an envelope. You might choose green paper or decorate your envelope with the color green somehow, as green is the color of the earth element and prosperity.

Gather some marjoram and nutmeg, both of which are prosperity herbs/spices. Also, get some cumin, which deters theft.

On your paper, draw a bill in the currency of the country where you will be vending. Then place a coin, preferably the largest denomination in the currency, under the paper. Rub a pencil or crayon over the coin so that you get an imprint of the coin on the paper.

If you are artistic, draw your vending table and many customers surrounding it.

Write the word *theft*, then write the word *shoplifting* under it. Draw a red circle with a line through it around these two words. This symbol is understood by the Universe.

Draw the symbol for the planet Mercury on the paper, as Mercury supports business ventures. Also, draw the symbol for Taurus, which is the fixed earth sign of the zodiac. Taurus is very much about the material world.

Now, in a blank space of the paper so that it is legible, write:

)))))●●●((((

At [name of event] I sell
Oh so very well
All goods are paid for
Big bills in the cash drawer
For the greatest good of all
So mote it be

)))))●●●((((

Put your paper in the envelope along with a pinch of marjoram, nutmeg, and cumin. Seal the envelope.

Take a deep breath, relax your body, and let any anxiety or dark energy get heavy and sink deep into the earth.

Visualize yourself at your vending table, your cash drawer overflowing with large bills and many customers in line that want to purchase your wares.

Pull energy from Mother Earth up through your feet and legs, up to your heart, and out through your projective hand. Draw down energy from the Universe through the top of your head, down to your heart, and out through your receptive hand. With your projective hand, draw an invoking pentagram over the envelope. See it sparkle in green, then visualize it energizing the envelope and its contents with green prosperity energy. Let any excess energy return to you through your receptive hand and ground it out through your feet.

Now infuse the envelope with the energy of Mercury. First, inhale deeply into your diaphragm and exhale, creating an empty space. Remember to ensure that your ego is not occupying that space. Then visualize the planet Mercury and pull the energy of Mercury into you. Remember that you are filling yourself with the energy of the planet.

Let the Mercury energy flow from your core out of your hands and eyes to the envelope holding your spell. With the power of Mercury flowing out of your hands, draw the symbol of Mercury over the envelope with your projective hand. Now visualize the business acumen and success of Mercury lighting up the envelope. Again, visualize yourself at the vending table with lots of successful sales.

Cross your arms in front of you and then open up as if you were opening up a coat; this devokes the Mercury energy from you.

If you have the opportunity to bury the envelope where it will not be found, do so. Otherwise, burn the envelope and, as you do so, visualize the intent being sent to the Universe.

Other Common Spell Techniques

As I mentioned previously, there exist a nearly infinite number of magical techniques for creating spells, such as magical waters and spell bags. In this chapter, I have picked just a few that I have found the most useful and come back to often. They can be adapted to fit your intent and needs.

Moon Water

Moon water is water that is magically charged by the moon. It can be used to add additional power to any cleansing, or you can add it to any spell that incorporates water.

Moon Water to Fortify Spells

YOU WILL NEED

Water, preferably rainwater or water from a stream or body of water, but tap water works

A jar with a lid

A night with a full moon

A place away from sunlight where you can store the jar

To make moon water, fill a jar with water. Rainwater is preferred, or water from a stream or other body of water. However, if you live in an arid climate and such water is challenging to obtain, you can use tap water; the moon will cleanse it.

Set the jar outside overnight during a full moon. When you wake in the morning, close the jar and bring it inside. Store it somewhere away from sunlight. Sun energy is different than moon energy, and you want this water to have pure moon energy.

Magical Holy Water

YOU WILL NEED

Water, preferably moon water

A cauldron or chalice

Salt

A bottle to store the water in

An athame (optional)

Place water in a cauldron or large chalice. If you can, use water that you have charged under the full moon. If you use an athame, dip it in salt and lift some salt with the tip of the athame. Put the athame and salt into the water. If you don't use an athame, grab a pinch of salt with your fingers and add it to the water. Repeat this twice more so that you have a total of three knife tips (or pinches) worth of salt in the water.

Bottle the water and store it somewhere away from the sun. Use this water for blessings or sprinkle it around as part of a house clearing. Sprinkle the water on any object that you are using in a spell.

Spell Bag

YOU WILL NEED

A piece of leather or material; chamois is popular for spell bags

Thread or string to close the bag with

Gemstones or other small objects that correspond with your intent

Herbs that support your intent

Incense that supports your intent

Matches or a lighter

Pen

Pentacle plate or a piece of paper with a pentacle drawn on it

Strainer

Body fluid, liquor, or perfume

Book of Shadows, grimoire, or magical notebook for documentation

To make a spell bag, select a piece of leather or other material in a color that supports your goal using the correspondences from chapter 5 or another color system that you work with. Chamois is often used as the material for a spell bag, but any material will work. Either sew the material into a bag shape or find a piece of string that is long enough to tie the piece of fabric together later.

Next, select the items that you want to include in your spell bag. Choose small items so that the bag does not become excessively heavy. Research herbs and include the dried versions. You can include other talismans and amulets in the bag; for example, to attract wealth, you could include lucky (found) coins. You can also write or draw what you want to manifest on a piece of paper and include that. Just as when creating a spell using runes, the number of items in the bag should be odd-numbered for the most power. Three items is the smallest number of items it should contain. Seven items are lucky, as are thirteen.

As for any spell, you can also include anything that is associated with the person who the spell is for. This is not strictly necessary, as the person will wear the spell bag.

Next, cleanse the bag and the items. For items that will not be destroyed by getting wet, bathe them in running water while visualizing red energy coming up from Mother Earth, through your feet, and to the heart as before. Visualize white or violet energy coming down from the Universe through the top of your head, mixing with the red energy at your heart. Send out rainbow, sparkling energy through your hands and through the item, then back up to your heart to complete the process. Remove the item from the water, then consecrate it and give it purpose by saying an incantation over it while continuously visualizing the energy flowing and your goal being achieved. Dry the item. Put it on a pentacle plate or a piece of paper with an encircled pentagram drawn on it while you cleanse and consecrate the rest of the items. To cleanse items that should not get wet, like dried herbs, you can put them in a strainer and cleanse with incense smoke.

Next, breathe life into the spell bag. You can do this by visualizing giving birth to the bag or by asking the Lady and the Lord to give the bag life. You can also breathe life into it while visualizing the bag supporting your goal and seeing your goal be accomplished. Giving life to the spell bag this way is similar to how you give life to a Thoughtform, which will be discussed in chapter 12.

Finally, tie or sew the bag shut and wear it where it cannot be seen. Like with all magic, you do not want to discuss your spell with someone who has not partaken in creating it, so do not invite questions by wearing it visibly!

Never let anyone else touch your spell bag. Once it is yours, it is yours only. "How does it become mine if someone else made it for me?" you may ask. You should give the spell bag spirit, *your* spirit, by adding a small amount of spirits (alcoholic beverages or perfume that contains alcohol) or bodily fluids to the outside of the bag. Dab it on.

Like a Thoughtform, the spell bag has life, and you need to care for it. You can dab fluids on it regularly to "feed" it. Alcohol that appropriate magical herbs have steeped in is an excellent choice!

Chapter 10

))»●●◖◖((C

POTIONS AND
KITCHEN MAGIC

No matter what kind of spell you are going to perform,
there are items in your kitchen that can be the heart
of the spell. At the very least, there are items in your
kitchen that can be used to layer the spell's magic.

To use herbs in spell work, you can roll oiled candles in herbs,
or you can fold a written spell into an envelope and put herbs in it,
or you can burn herbs as an incense while you perform your spell.
Certain herbs can be made into infusions (tea) and drank as part
of the spell work. Healing herbs can be crushed and stirred into a
mixture of melted beeswax and olive oil for a salve.

In this chapter, I will share more ways to use what you find in
your kitchen.

Food Magic

In chapter 5, I shared some foods and their correspondences. This is a great chapter to refer back to when planning your spell work. In addition to eating foods whose correspondences match your spell's goal, use herbs. You can make herbal tea and bless it with your goal, then drink it, just as you would for any cup of tea. You can add herbs to the culinary dishes that you make. Some herbs make a lovely liquor if you steep them in vodka and add sugar.

Just as you can add herbs and foodstuffs to various types of spells for layering, you can also create spells that are centered around the edible. This section shares some examples of such spells. Remember, always check that your ingredients are safe to ingest in the way that you are preparing them.

Spells Using Infusions

An infusion is similar to a tea. You create an infusion by pouring simmering water over leaves or stems in a cup or mug. As you do so, say an incantation that you have written for this purpose, visualize your goal as having manifested, and draw an invoking pentagram over the cup to activate the herbs' magical properties into the infusion. Let the infusion steep until you feel that the magic has been established. Once it's ready, you can either drink the tea while again saying your incantation and visualizing your goal, or you can use the infusion as part of another type of spell work. If you are going to ingest the infusion, be certain to verify that the plants are safe to consume.

Spells Using Decoctions

A decoction is similar to an infusion, but the substance is boiled rather than steeped. You can prepare leaves, stems, berries, or fruit this way. Dried fruits and berries work very well when prepared in this way. Use a decoction the same way you use an infusion. Beware that a decoction can be very strong, so that you might wish to dilute it if you are going to drink it.

Spells Using Macerated Fruits and Berries

I love this method! Let fruits and berries soak in wine or hard liquor, or simply put the berries or fruit in a bowl of sugar. Read your incantation over the fruits or berries as you start the process. Wait thirty minutes and see how much liquid is in the bowl. If there is not very much liquid after about thirty minutes, add wine or liquor. (If you're doing this method using dried fruits, this process will need to sit overnight.) In any case, the results are very soft fruit and a liquid sauce. Spoon it over vanilla ice cream and eat it while visualizing your goal manifested, or add just a few berries or pieces of fruit to a glass of wine, then simply drink the wine with the intent of manifesting your goal.

Spells Using Mulled Wine

Similar to the previous method, but not the same, is mulled wine. Pick appropriate spices for one of your goals and boil these spices in a small amount of wine for about an hour. Take the pan off the heat, add additional wine, and add sugar to taste. If you need to heat your concoction, do so very carefully. Feel free to spike it with a liquor of your choice, one that supports the manifestation of your goal. Sip the drink slowly while focusing on the goal being manifest.

Spells Using Tinctures

To make a tincture, place edible herbs and spices that support your goal into a bottle. If you are using fresh herbs, ensure that they are thoroughly cleaned first. Splash a little hot water inside, then fill the bottle up with high-proof liquor. It needs to be at least 80 proof; 100 proof is better (at least 40 percent ABV; 50 percent ABV is better). The higher the alcohol content of the liquor you use, the safer you are from anything going wrong with your tincture (e.g., mold).

A tincture is strong in alcohol! Use it as a base for a mixed drink, add it to a spell bag, put a few drops under your tongue using a dropper, or add a few drops to a sauce. Please ensure that the taste of your tincture is compatible with the method you choose to use.

Some practitioners make tinctures with apple cider vinegar. I stay away, as I feel that liquor is a safer choice, as bacteria and mold do not grow in alcohol stronger than 20 percent ABV, or 40 proof.

Fire in Spell Work

Many of the spell methods that are described in this book involve burning something. A very traditional fire for spell work is made with isopropyl alcohol (rubbing alcohol) and Epsom salt—91 percent isopropyl alcohol is the best choice; 70 percent rubbing alcohol is not as easy to work with for this purpose.

Exercise: Small Fire Indoors

You will need

Isopropyl alcohol, 91 percent or higher

Epsom salt

A fireproof container (e.g., a cast-iron cauldron)

A heatproof surface (e.g., a trivet)

A spoon or other device to measure ingredients with

A long (fireplace) match

Mix equal amounts of isopropyl alcohol and Epsom salt in a fireproof container. A common choice for this is a small cast-iron cauldron, but any fireproof container will do. Make sure that the container is on a heatproof surface, such as a trivet. The container will get extremely hot and will burn the surface it is on if not protected.

When mixing your isopropyl alcohol and Epsom salt, start with small amounts. I recommend starting with one tablespoon of each. Once you have some experience, you can, of course, make a larger and longer-burning fire.

Light the fire with a long (fireplace) match. The fire will light as soon as you put the match to the alcohol, but it is sometimes hard to see the flames in the beginning. With a short match, you risk burning your hands.

You will notice Epsom salt residue in the container when the fire has died out; you can dispose of this in the trash or bury it.

Chapter 11

)))))●●●((((

AMULETS AND TALISMANS

The meanings of the words *amulet* and *talisman* differ between practitioners. In some practices, amulets protect against evil and danger whereas talismans manifest a specific benefit. In other cases, amulets are defined as being created by someone for a particular purpose whereas talismans are natural objects not adulterated. And then, other people define amulets as being made only with natural objects whereas talismans are created by a person, often at astrologically significant times. Think about which approach makes sense to you.

I believe that an amulet is any object with symbols or properties against evil that is then worn. Talismans manifest a specific benefit. Here are some common examples of talismans:

An Ankh: Wearing the ankh symbol on your person brings long life and vitality.

A Spell Bag: As described in chapter 9, spell bags can be worn for many types of spell work.

A Small Thoughtform: Creating a Thoughtform is discussed in chapter 12.

Crystals That Are Worn: Wear crystals in a wire cage or as jewelry, or carry them in your pocket. Wearing the crystal gives you the specific benefits of that crystal.

A Small Piece of Baked Clay: The clay should have an inscription that works with your goal.

The Ankh

The ankh can be both an amulet and a talisman. Which category it falls in depends on the intent of the wearer. For example, some may wear it both for health and vitality and to ward off evil, in which case the same object serves as both a talisman and an amulet.

Crystals as Amulets or Talismans

If you'd like to use crystals as an amulet or talisman, research the magical properties of the crystal and ensure it is are not toxic to touch.

Here is a very rough guide to the magical properties of gemstones:

- Black stones are typically grounding. Examples are black tourmaline, hematite, and obsidian. (Note: obsidian is not technically a crystal, as it is glass formed from lava, but it carries magical energy like a crystal.)

- Red stones are also grounding and help you manifest what you desire. They also support stamina and stability in life, including economic security. Examples are red jasper, garnet, and ruby.

- Orange stones typically support joie de vivre and increase libido. Usually, they help you sort out your feelings instead of suppressing them. Orange stones can also help with family relationships. Examples are carnelian and amber. (Again, amber is technically not a crystal. It is a resin, but it carries magical energy like a crystal.)

- Yellow stones and brownish-yellow stones typically help with ambition, willpower, setting boundaries, and action in general. Examples are tiger's eye and citrine.

- Green stones and pink stones typically help with self-love, love in relationships, harmony within groups, and manifesting friends or a group membership. Examples are bloodstone, green kyanite, kunzite, and rose quartz.

- Blue stones typically help with diplomacy, speaking freely and clearly, eloquence, and being truthful. Examples are blue kyanite, lapis lazuli, and sodalite.

- Dark purple and very dark blue stones typically help with intellectual undertakings and clairvoyance, clairaudience, channeling, contacting spirits, ESP, and mental health. Examples are purple fluorite and amethyst, which can also be used for sobriety.

- Light purple, clear, and white stones typically help with spirituality, connection with deity, and finding the divine within. Examples are diamond, Herkimer diamond (a form of clear quartz), clear quartz, and selenite.

This list is, of course, an overly generalized categorization, but it is beneficial as a guide.

Before wearing stones for magical use, you should cleanse them and charge them. Cleansing can be done in running water, in incense smoke, by burying in salt (if it will not damage the stone), soaking in salt water (if it will not damage the stone), or by burying in dirt. Keeping crystals near citrine and kyanite will also cleanse them. Citrine and kyanite are the only two stones that cannot absorb negative energy and never need cleansing. Charging can be done by leaving the stone to soak up the moonlight or by leaving it to sit on your altar, if you have one, for at least several days.

You can wear stones in a variety of ways. As amulets or talismans, you would wear the stone in a wire cage, wrapped with wire, or in another setting that allows it to act as a pendant. Many stones can be found on beaded necklaces or bracelets. If you don't want to wear crystals as jewelry, you can include smaller stones in a spell bag, or you can simply keep the stones in your pocket. If you wear a bra, you can put polished rocks in your bra. Rough crystals tend to get uncomfortable quickly when stuffed in a bra!

Exercise: Find Supporting Crystals

You will need

A source that lists the magical properties of crystals; if not available, use the list provided here as a guide

Actual, physical crystals (optional)

For one of your goals, identify three different crystals that support the goal. Then, if feasible, acquire the stones, cleanse them, consecrate them, and wear them.

Inscribed Clay Pendant

Making your own magical items is powerful because you imbue them with the exact properties that you need for your intent. Making and inscribing a clay pendant is easy and relatively quick.

Exercise: Inscribed Clay Pendant

YOU WILL NEED

The objective of the pendant

Oven-bake clay or no-bake clay

A leather string or a string made of another strong material to hold the pendant

A tool to inscribe the clay with

Book of Shadows, grimoire, or magical notebook for documentation

Roll the clay to about one-eighth inch thick. Cut out a circle the size of a US quarter. This will be your pendant. Make a hole near the edge of the pendant that is large enough to put a leather string through. (Do not add the string yet.) With a pointed object, such as a fine knitting needle, inscribe the clay with an incantation that describes the purpose of the amulet or talisman while focusing on your intent. Depending on what type of clay you used, bake the pendant in the oven or air-dry it. Once the clay has hardened and cooled, string the leather string through and wear your pendant as a necklace.

Chapter 12

)))◗●●◖(((

THOUGHTFORMS

Thoughtform is a creation of yours that you have given life,
a name, and a specific task or purpose. Thoughtforms are
useful when you need a spell to work continuously over
an extended period of time, e.g., protecting your home or giving
you the strength to stick to a healthy diet.

Thoughtforms can be merely energetic or they can reside in an
object, often a statue. Broadly, a Thoughtform is created when you
visualize its appearance and concentrate on its purpose. Instilling
your emotions into a Thoughtform can help solidify its purpose.
Your thoughts, concentration, and emotions move a Thoughtform
from existing only in your consciousness to existing as an independent entity, capable of agency. The stronger your emotions are, the
stronger and more powerful the Thoughtform will be. Emotion is
a potent force!

To create a Thoughtform, first define its purpose. Think about why you are making a Thoughtform. Be precise and define what you want it to accomplish. Next, write down the Thoughtform's purpose in your Book of Shadows or magical journal. It is easy to forget, and you may need to deprogram the Thoughtform eventually if you have not limited its lifetime.

Once you've written down the Thoughtform's purpose, write an incantation for each of the elements. Make sure each incantation describes the elemental aspect of the Thoughtform's purpose.

Think about what name you will give your Thoughtform. The name can be an acronym for its purpose or a shortened form of its purpose, or it can have any name that you find suitable. Research the meaning and connotations of the name to ensure that it will not conflict with the purpose of the Thoughtform. Please do not assign it the name yet; you will name your Thoughtform during its creation ritual.

Next, decide whether you want your Thoughtform to reside in an object or be purely energetic. Thoughtforms that are to act in the nearby area do well when living in things; Thoughtforms whose magic has to act far away work best when purely energetic. The next two sections will explain how to finish creating your Thoughtform, depending on which method you choose.

Creating a Thoughtform in an Object

If you want your Thoughtform to reside in an object, here are a few steps to take prior to creating it:

- Get some dirt or cornmeal to cleanse the object. You can use salt, but remember it will cleanse the object completely of any and all energies, even good energy. If you use salt and another substance, you must use the salt first, as it will negate anything and everything you have done before its use. During your Thoughtform's creation ritual, you are going to rub dirt, cornmeal, or salt on the object and bless it with the element of earth. At that time, you will also state the length of its life and make it stable in this realm.

- Find an essential oil that supports your purpose. During your Thoughtform's creation ritual, you will use this to anoint the object and bless it with the element of fire. You will give it its mission and the drive to fulfill it.

- Find a tea that supports your purpose or make a potion using corresponding herbs. During your Thoughtform's creation ritual, you will use this to asperge the object and bless it with the element of water. This will give it empathy, compassion, and ethics.

- Find an incense that supports your purpose. You will use this to smoke the object and bless it with the element of air. This will give your Thoughtform the intellect to go about its tasks in a well-thought-out manner.

- Find as many items that support your goal as possible. You will be presenting these items to the Thoughtform as a tribute and to layer the magic. You can lay the items in front of the Thoughtform or attach them to it, so you could gather feathers, crystals, books, pendants, amulets, talismans, cords, or any corresponding object that supports your goal.

Once you have gathered all of the appropriate items and fully visualized your Thoughtform, you are ready to perform the creation ritual.

Object-Based Thoughtform

YOU WILL NEED

An object to hold the Thoughtform

Elemental incantations

A substance that symbolizes earth (e.g., soil)

An oil that supports your intent

A potion / tea made with herbs that support the intent of the
Thoughtform

An incense that supports the intent

Matches or a lighter

Tributes that support your intent, to be given to the
Thoughtform

Pen

Book of Shadows, grimoire, or magical notebook for
documentation

First, cleanse the object you have chosen to hold the Thought-form with incense, salt, water, or fire.

While visualizing the Thoughtform, concentrate on its purpose, and focus on your emotions around that purpose. At the same time, rub the substance you have chosen to represent earth onto the object. Recite an appropriate earth-related incantation to support the purpose of the Thoughtform. This incantation should provide the Thoughtform grounding energy and include an end date for its existence; this will establish its lifetime.

Rub the selected oil on the object while reciting an appropriate fire-related incantation for your Thoughtform. This incantation should be worded to give it power and passion for its purpose.

Rub the prepared potion on the item while reciting an appropriate water-related incantation. This incantation should ensure that the Thoughtform works ethically and is compassionate.

Wave the object in the smoke of your selected incense while reciting an appropriate air-related incantation. This incantation should ensure that the Thoughtform works logically and rationally.

Finally, call upon Spirit or your chosen deity, while saying, "I call upon the Spirit to infuse this Thoughtform with the ability to act for the greatest good of all."

Put your first tribute to the Thoughtform in front of it (or attach it) while saying, "I present to you this [tribute]. As I give you this [tribute], I [your intent]."

Repeat for each item you are presenting or attaching to the Thoughtform.

Once you've finished offering your tributes, chant the key concept of the purpose of the Thoughtform. Chant the purpose repeatedly; you will know when to stop, as you will feel the power peak.

Once power has peaked, breathe life into the Thoughtform. Visualize it coming to life while saying, "I call you into being, and I give you the name [name], which I give you so that [reason you chose that name]." Chant the name many times over. Don't stop chanting the name until you sense that the Thoughtform is responding and knows its name.

Release the Thoughtform to fulfill its programming while saying, "Go forth, [name]. Bring us [the purpose of the Thoughtform]. So mote it be!"

Chapter 12

Creating a Purely Energetic Thoughtform

Creating a purely energetic Thoughtform is similar to creating a Thoughtform in an object, so I will only describe the process briefly.

If your Thoughtform is going to be purely energetic, decide on what its form is. Ask yourself questions along the lines of:

- What does it look like?
- Is it humanlike? Is it animallike? Is it just a shape?
- Does it wear clothes? If so, what clothes?
- What color is it?
- Is it a mechanical item? For example, does it look like R2D2?

If you are artistic, draw or paint the Thoughtform. Put the picture in your Book of Shadows or magical journal. In any case, be certain that you have a clear picture of how it looks.

Energetic-Only Thoughtform

YOU WILL NEED

A place to work undisturbed

Once you have decided what your Thoughtform looks like, visualize yourself giving birth to the Thoughtform or visualize the Thoughtform materializing in front of you. Again, concentrate on its purpose and the emotions you have toward it.

Call upon the elements to give the Thoughtform existence on this plane and breathe spirit into it. This step is the creation of the Thoughtform.

Say the name of the Thoughtform and its instructions; repeat three times. This is how to program the Thoughtform.

Release the Thoughtform to fulfill its programming while saying, "Go forth, [name]. Bring us [the purpose of the Thoughtform]. So mote it be!"

Creating Thoughtforms in a Group Setting

Some people chose to create Thoughtforms in a group setting because there is a lot of power in having many minds working on establishing the same result. However, there could be a lot of chaos if those minds don't agree on the mechanism that will create that result. Coherence is, in this case, the difference between successful magic and failed magic.

Creating a Thoughtform in a group setting has some extra challenges. Everyone in the group must have the same concept of what the Thoughtform looks like and agree on its exact purpose. Otherwise, you will end up creating a jumbled mess that is incapable of functioning. As a group, decide what the astral manifestation of the Thoughtform looks like. You need to agree on both its purpose and the mechanism for the Thoughtform to manifest that purpose. Since emotions are also part of creating the Thoughtform, you need to thoroughly inquire how each individual in the group feels about the Thoughtform itself and its purpose. Ensure that you have consistency of emotions within the group before creating the Thoughtform.

Examples of Thoughtforms

Thoughtforms are a somewhat complex concept, and therefore I will give several examples of how to create different Thoughtforms.

Candle Magic as a Thoughtform

Candle magic comes in many forms. Peace in a candle is a Thoughtform that manifests peace in times of turbulence.

Peace in a Candle

YOU WILL NEED

A candleholder

A candle as a tribute

Matches or a lighter

Dry soil

Corresponding oil

Corresponding potion / tea

Corresponding incense

Wiccan Rede (can be found online)

A piece of amethyst

A piece of hematite

The object that will be the home for the Thoughtform is the candleholder.

Rub dry soil onto the candleholder while stating, "I call upon the element of earth to infuse this Thoughtform with stability and endurance to maintain peace in this time of upheaval."

Rub the selected oil on the candleholder while stating, "I call upon the element of fire to infuse this Thoughtform with the courage and daring required to maintain peace in this time of upheaval."

Rub the prepared potion on the candleholder while stating, "I call upon the element of water to infuse this Thoughtform with the emotion and compassion required to maintain peace in this time of upheaval."

Wave the candleholder in the smoke of the selected incense while stating, "I call upon the element of air to infuse this Thoughtform with the intelligence and comprehension required to maintain peace in this time of upheaval."

To ensure the greatest good of all, finish by saying, "I call upon Spirit to infuse this Thoughtform with the ability to act within the limits of the words from the Wiccan Rede." Recite the Rede, ending with, "For the greatest good of all, so mote it be."

Now it is time to program the Thoughtform. Put the candle in the holder and state, "I give to you this candle. As I light this candle with my flame, I bind you to me and me to you."

Place a small piece of amethyst in front of the candleholder and state, "I present you with the calming power of amethyst, that you may calm the emotions that arise around you."

Place a small piece of hematite in front of the candleholder and state, "I present you with this hematite for peace, control, and inner happiness."

Chant the key concept of the purpose of the Thoughtform ("Peace, peace, peace") repeatedly. You will know when to stop, as you will feel the power peak.

Once power has peaked, breathe life into the Thoughtform. Visualize it coming to life while stating, "I call you into being, and I give you the name Fred, which means peace in the Scandinavian languages." The name is pronounced like Freyd, but as if you removed the y just before pronouncing the d. Pronouncing it in the Scandinavian way ensures that the name itself will layer the magic with its meaning. Chant the name many times, until you sense that the Thoughtform responds and knows that it is Fred.

Release the Thoughtform to fulfill its programming while stating, "Go forth, Fred. Bring us peace. Bring us peace. So mote it be!"

Light the candle. You don't have to let the candle burn down fully; the candle is a tribute and also connects the two of you. You can light it whenever you wish to remind yourself of the purpose of Fred. When the candle is nearly fully burned, light another candle from the original before you extinguish the original. Put the new candle in the holder and continue doing this with each candle as it nears the end. This way, you have an unbroken chain.

Prodeety: A Thoughtform for PROtection from Dogs EntEring The Yard

Suppose that you have had a problem with stray dogs entering your yard. You do not know if they are vaccinated, and they are also causing a sanitary issue. You want them to stay out. Thus, you create a Thoughtform to keep the stray dogs at bay. This exercise will talk you through how I created this Thoughtform.

YOU WILL NEED

A place to work undisturbed

Bowl of soil

Bowl with drops of corresponding oil in a carrier oil

Corresponding incense

Matches or a lighter

Corresponding potion

This energetic-only Thoughtform is a male three-headed dog, Prodeety. His name is a shortened form of his purpose; his purpose is to (PRO)tect from (D)ogs (E)nt(E)ring (T)he (Y)ard.

Prodeety is enormous, and he is black with a single white spot on his left flank. In addition to his fearsome looks, he has a strong scent that only dogs can smell. To other dogs, the smell acts as a deterrent from entering the yard.

Visualize Prodeety taking shape in front of you. Then hold up a bowl of soil and state, "I call upon the element of earth to infuse this Thoughtform with the stability and endurance required to keep stray dogs out of the yard."

Hold up a small bowl with a few drops of appropriate essential oil in a carrier oil. State, "I call upon the element of fire to infuse this Thoughtform with the courage and daring required to keep stray dogs out of the yard."

Pour some of the prepared potion on the ground or into a bowl before the visualized Thoughtform. State, "I call upon the element of water to infuse this Thoughtform with the emotion and compassion required to keep stray dogs out of the yard."

Wave the smoke from the selected incense in front of the visualized Thoughtform while stating, "I call upon the element of air to infuse this Thoughtform with the intelligence and comprehension required to keep stray dogs out of the yard."

Finally, say, "I call upon Spirit to infuse this Thoughtform with the ability to act for the greatest good of all."

Now breathe life spirit into your Thoughtform. Visualize him coming to life—see him breathing and moving. Tell him, "I name you Prodeety. You are Prodeety, that is your name. Your name is Prodeety."

Then repeat this three times, chanting with increasing intensity: "Prodeety, three-headed, fearsome, and dear to us dog, the yard belongs to you, and only you. Other dogs do not belong. Keep them out." On the third and final repetition, shout the word *out*.

Then let Prodeety out in the yard. Focus intently on seeing him in the yard, keeping other dogs away.

Creating a Coyote Thoughtform for Protection

The need for security is universal. This example is a Thoughtform in the shape of a coyote, used for personal protection.

YOU WILL NEED

No-bake or oven-bake clay for earth

Dragon's blood essential oil for fire

A protective potion for water (e.g., an infusion made from bay leaf, caraway seeds, cloves, and garlic)

A protective incense for air (e.g., frankincense fortified with myrrh)

Matches or a lighter

Pentagram

Tiger's eye crystal

Wooden figa

Silver bracelet

Acorn

Black opal

Start by shaping a piece of clay into the form of a coyote to the best of your ability. The clay represents earth. Place your hands on the clay form and bless it by saying, "I call upon the power of the coyote; he who burrows in the ground, he who has vision through the darkness, he who howls in the night. With the element of earth, I create thee to defend and protect me from evil and malevolent energies."

Next, anoint the clay statue with the dragon's blood oil and state, "I call upon the power of coyote, ferocious predator, skilled hunter, presenter of fire. With the element of fire, I create thee to defend and protect me from malevolent energies."

Then, anoint the statue with an appropriately brewed potion and state, "I call upon the power of coyote, friend of the badger, friend of the eagle, mate of the wolf. With the element of water, I create thee to defend and protect me from malevolent energies."

Wave the statue through smoke from an appropriately blended incense and say, "I call upon the power of coyote; he who is inventive, he who is mischievous, he who readily learns from others. With the element of air, I create thee to defend and protect me from malevolent energies."

Program the Thoughtform as follows:

- "I present you with this pentagram. As you wear this sacred symbol, it connects you to me and me to you, just as I have worn it to connect with the Lady and the Lord."
- "I give you the power of tiger's eye so that you may have strength."
- "I give you the power of the wooden figa for strength and protection so that you may have power and power to share."
- "I give you the power of the silver bracelet so that you may be self-assured and infuse me with the same."
- "I give you the power of acorn so that you may be strong and sturdy as an oak and can share your strength without tiring."
- "I give you the power of the black opal so that you may transform your fears into energy and optimism and spread the strength without loss."

Chant the key concept of the purpose of the Thoughtform ("Strength, energy, determination") repeatedly. You will know when to stop; you will feel the power peak.

Breathe life into the Thoughtform and visualize it coming to life. Say, "I impart you with Spirit, bring you into being, and I name you [name]." Chant the name many times over until you sense that the Thoughtform knows its name and responds.

Release the Thoughtform to fulfill its programming by saying, "[Name], go forth! Bring strength, energy, and determination! So mote it be!"

Thoughtform as an Amulet or Talisman

A thoughtform can reside in a small physical object just as well as in a large one. You can establish a Thoughtform in an object that is small enough to be worn as a talisman or amulet. As discussed in chapter 11, amulets protect against evil and danger whereas talismans manifest a specific benefit.

Deprogramming a Thoughtform

When you create a Thoughtform, it is essential that you document what you programmed it to do and how you went about that programming.

Maybe what you programmed it to do is something that, at some point, becomes contrary to what you need at the time, and you need to deprogram the Thoughtform. To deprogram a Thoughtform, you need to reverse what you did to program it, and if you don't have it written down, chances are that you will struggle with the deprogramming, and therefore, there will be remnants of the programming left. Those remnants can cause major headaches!

To reverse the programming in a Thoughtform that is housed in an object, first call the Thoughtform back into the object in case it is drifting around nearby. A Thoughtform in an object can never be far away, so all you need to do is call to it by saying something along the lines of, "[Name of Thoughtform], I call you back into your abode, your home, this [object where it resides] where you reside." Next, thank the Thoughtform for the work that it has done, e.g., "[Name of Thoughtform], your work is complete, and I thank you for all that you have done. I will send you now to become one again with your brethren and sisters, without any tasks or duties." Continue by removing each item you had given the Thoughtform. (If you gave an item to tie the two of you together, leave it for last.) For each item you remove, state your thanks: "I thank you for the good use you have made of the [item] during your time of duty." As I remove this [item], you are freed from the burden of carrying the power of [power that the item imbued on the Thoughtform]. That power is now removed from you."

Once you have removed any item that tied you together, remove the name that you gave to the Thoughtform by saying, "You have done your duty with honor, and you are freed from being [name]. There is no [name]." Then inhale and take back the life that you gave to the Thoughtform by saying, "I thank you again, and I bring you out of being. This here is just an [object]."

If the Thoughtform is purely energetic, the deprogramming follows the same steps, except that you first visualize the Thought-form as being in the room with you and call it home to you. Next, thank the Thoughtform for the work that it has done, e.g., "[Name of Thoughtform], your work is complete, and I thank you for all that you have done. I will send you now to become one again with your brethren and sisters, without any tasks or duties." End by say-ing, "The Thoughtform that was called [name] is no more."

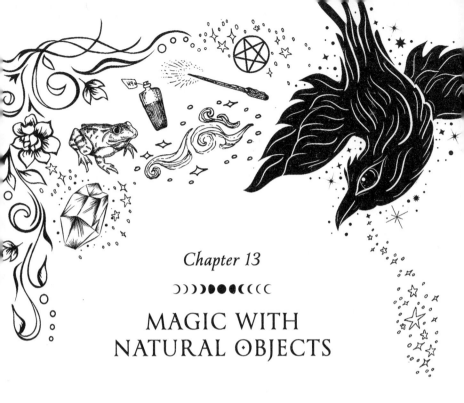

Chapter 13

))))❂●◗◖((((

MAGIC WITH
NATURAL ❂BJECTS

Many objects that are found in nature lend themselves naturally to magic. Sticks and stones and pelts and bones have intrinsic magical properties of the tree, mineral, or animal from which they came. The same holds true for shells.

There are stores where you can purchase ethically sourced bones and pelts, and there are also options online. Make sure that you know how these types of objects were sourced. An animal that was killed for its bones or fur may not be inclined to work with you.

Spells Using Bones and Pelts

Spells using bones and pelts rely on the Law of Contagion to allow you to work with the spirit of the animal from which they came.

Such spells are not the same as shamanic work, which is working with a power animal or working with spirit animals. Spells with bones and pelts are more akin to working with your ancestors, but instead, you are working with the spirit of a specific animal. Sometimes the connection will even let you draw on the entire species and the archetype it stands for.

You can use bones or pelts to layer most types of spells. For example, add a piece of bone or a part of the pelt to a paper spell, a jar spell, a cord spell, etc.

You can also do spells that solely work with the spirit of the animal whose bones or fur you are using. If, for example, you want the animal to protect a valuable object of yours, place the bone(s) or pelt on the object and politely ask the animal to protect the item for you. State an incantation indicating that the animal is protecting the object. Animal skulls are particularly powerful for this sort of magic.

If you want to acquire the properties of the animal whose pelt you have, wear the pelt with the fur side out. Then, politely ask the animal to be with you and share its properties with you.

Always thank the animal when using bones or pelts in spell work.

It is prudent to be careful when finding out what an animal stands for. Some characteristics are more or less universal (e.g., the wisdom of the owl), and these are the ones for which the magic is the most successful. Understandings shared by many are more accessible to magical workings than those known only by a few. A few common animal characteristics, besides the owl, are:

Bear: Comfort; caring for children; introspection, as they hibernate; good fishing luck, as they are expert fishers; strength

Cow: Prosperity, as they give milk, meat, and more cows

Ermine or Weasel: Speed; ability to hide; staying mysterious; stealth; ermine is also associated with worldly power, as it has been commonly worn by royalty

Fox: Being sly

Horse: Loyalty; intelligence

Lion: Courage; strength

Moose (in Some Places Elk or Large Species of Deer): King of the forest, as they are the largest animal around

Rabbit: Fertility, because rabbits keep making many more rabbits; rabbits are also associated with jumping ahead

Squirrel: Preparing for the days ahead, as they store nuts for the winter

Spells Using Shells

All shells are protective, as they protect the mollusk inside. Shells can be used either as the focal point in a protection spell or to enhance one.

Spells Using Snail Shells

The shell of a snail is its home and its protection. It follows that snail shells are protective and can also be used to find new housing.

Ground snail shells can be added to spell bags, paper spells, or any type of spell that will hold a powder. Whole shells can be added to spell bags, as long as they're small. Snail shells can be added to witch's ladders. Whole shells can be strung into a necklace if you carefully drill holes for the string. As you string the necklace, do so with the intent of protecting yourself or finding a new home.

Spells Using Cowrie Shells

Cowries are sea snails and are typically very shiny and beautiful. Their shells have historically been used as currency and as jewelry.[6] Therefore, they are a symbol of prosperity. They also bring good luck. Because the underside of a cowrie shell somewhat resembles a vulva, they are also associated with female sexuality and fertility.

Cowrie shells should be used whole, as their beauty and shape are part of their magic. They can be used in all the ways that a snail shell can be used, except for ground.

Spells Using Scallop Shells

Scallop shells are, among other things, sacred to Aphrodite. Thus, if you want to feel sexier or be more erotic, write your intent on a piece of paper and place it on a scallop shell while visualizing yourself as you wish to feel.

Scallop shells are also catalysts. They significantly enhance other shell magic. Place a spell that incorporates snail shells or cowrie shells on a scallop shell to layer and strengthen the magic.

Spells Using Zebra Mussel Shells

I have highly mixed feelings about using zebra mussel shells in magic, yet I do it. It took me a while to come to understand that as much as I detest them, they are mighty creatures. Zebra mussels are invasive, and it takes just one contaminated boat to infest an entire lake. These mussels can also spread via waterfowl, so it is nearly impossible to stop their rampaging. If your intent is to be indomitable, unstoppable, and unconquerable, the zebra mussel shell is for you.

---

6. Hogendorn and Johnson, *Shell Money of the Slave Trade*.

If you are near waters that have been infested, zebra mussels are easy enough to find on the underside of dry-docked boats or on anything that has been in the water for more than a few days. You may wish to wear gloves, as the shells are sharp. Be careful.

Seed Spells

Seed spells are the spells to use if you have a green thumb. If you don't, you might want to skip this particular kind of magic. The concept is simple: a seed grows to a seedling and then to a full-grown plant, and when that growing power is associated with a spell for something you want to manifest, it will transfer the power of the growth to your goal.

Seed Spell

YOU WILL NEED

Pen

Paper

Book of Shadows, grimoire, or magical notebook for
    documentation

Flowerpot

Potting soil

Seed of a plant that you already know how to grow

Write an incantation for a goal of yours on a piece of paper. Draw any symbols that support the goal. Then fold the paper and put it in the bottom of a flowerpot. Fill the pot with soil and plant a seed that you are familiar with. As you plant the seed, visualize your goal being manifest. Please tend to your plant carefully!

Part Four

))))●●●(((C

SPELLS FOR
EVERY NEED

Chapter 14

))))●●●(((

QUICK SPELLS

Sometimes you don't need a big, elaborate spell; you just need to do something quickly to increase your chances of success for something you are about to do. As with all magic, the key to quick spells is to visualize the situation the way you want it to happen.

Spell for Success in Something That You Are Just About to Do

YOU WILL NEED

Unobstructed room to move forward on your timeline

Place yourself on your timeline when the event that you want to influence is going to take place. Place yourself in your body at that future time. In your mind, play out interactions with any others who will be present. Then step back to your now, put your hands together, and shake them quickly back and forth to raise energy. Visualize success and send the energy you just raised forward to the appropriate point in time. Say out loud or to yourself, "For the greatest good of all, so mote it be!"

Morning Spell for a Good Day

You will need

A food or beverage that you consume in the morning

When you prepare your coffee, tea, orange juice, or other morning beverage, smile and don't let go of the smile. Say, "Today is a good day, so I say" or a similar incantation. Then, with your index finger, draw an invoking pentagram over the cup or glass. If you don't consume a beverage in the morning, do this over your breakfast dish.

Anytime Spell for Clearing and Protection

You will need

Only yourself

Suppose you don't have the time to do a complete house clearing and set wards. In that case, you can protect yourself temporarily by first stating out loud, "Monsters and bad spirits begone. You are not welcome here. I tell you *go!* Now, disappear!" or a similar incantation. Draw a banishing pentagram while you say it. As soon as you have completed your incantation, visualize a shield around the area that you are in, as described in chapter 17.

Protection Against Anything Coming at You

YOU WILL NEED

Only yourself

This is one of the very first spells I learned from a teacher, and I use it frequently. Anytime you see something approaching you that you do not wish to come any closer, draw a banishing pentagram in the air with your hand or finger. Pull up energy from the earth to charge it as you visualize it glowing an electric blue. Then grab the visualization with your hand and throw it toward what is approaching you.

This spell is quick and effective, but it does require experience to get the pentagram charged properly. If it does not work the first time, keep practicing, and focus especially on how you charge the pentagram with energy from the earth.

This spell does not hurt whatever it is coming toward you, it only banishes it from the path that leads to you. I have used this spell against wasps, scary animals, and people. Remember, it is always ethical to protect yourself.

Chapter 15

)))) ● ● ● ((((

SPELLS FOR HEALING

Many of the spell types already discussed work well for healing. This chapter will share some additional details specifically for recovery and healing.

Using Crystals for Healing

Crystals have many uses in magic. One of the most common is for healing. In this section, I will describe a standard method—the same one that I use—for healing with crystals.

Cleansing of Crystals

When you bring a new stone home, you need to cleanse any negative energies it may have acquired before you found it. You should also cleanse crystals after you use them, to release any energies they may have picked up during your work.

There are many ways to cleanse a crystal. (The most common are mentioned in the section on using crystals as amulets.) I keep my working stones inside a circle of citrine and kyanite so that they are always ready. Once your stones are cleansed, they're ready to work with you.

Healing with Crystals

Healing with crystals is based on the chakra system. We discussed chakra basics in chapter 5, so this section will focus on which issues each chakra is associated with. The chakra system determines which stones clear certain issues. Specific crystals balance and heal each chakra; some crystals heal several chakras. Here is a summary of those aspects of the chakras:

> **Root Chakra Issues:** Illnesses of the feet and legs, constipation, eating disorders, hemorrhoids, fear and anxiety, poor eating habits, lack of exercise, lack of stability in life, spaciness, hoarding, inability to manifest goals

> **Root Chakra Stones:** Heal the root chakra with red stones and black stones such as red jasper, garnet, ruby, black tourmaline, obsidian, bloodstone, fire agate, red calcite, red aventurine, onyx, and red tiger's eye

> **Sacral Chakra Issues:** Reproductive system issues, lack of libido, overactive libido, being overemotional, being unfeeling, denying yourself pleasure, being addicted to fun and enjoyment, lack of creativity, being too out-of-the-box for reality, lack of joy in life

> **Sacral Chakra Stones:** Heal with orange stones such as carnelian, fire opal, amber, red aventurine, and orange calcite

Solar Plexus Chakra Issues: Issues with the digestive system or gallbladder, being domineering, being overly submissive, lack of limits and boundaries, lack of willpower, addiction, lack of drive, being too ambitious, being excessively competitive, aggression

Solar Plexus Chakra Stones: Heal with yellow stones such as yellow tiger's eye, citrine, pyrite, yellow topaz, and yellow jasper

Heart Chakra Issues: Heart and lung issues, depression, inability to form friendships or loving relationships, fear of developing loving relationships, over-giving, neglecting self, depending on someone else's happiness for your own (codependency)

Heart Chakra Stones: Heal with green stones or pink stones such as rose quartz, aventurine, moss agate, emerald, unakite, peridot, jade, malachite, and prehnite

Throat Chakra Issues: Issues with the throat/neck or shoulders, inability to express thoughts well, being tongue-tied, shyness, inability to state desires or opinions, excessive talking without conveying anything, speaking too loudly

Throat Chakra Stones: Heal with blue stones such as sodalite, lapis lazuli, turquoise, aquamarine, amazonite, and blue lace agate

Third Eye Chakra Issues: Headaches, vision problems, being unrealistic, living in fantasyland, hallucinations, bad dreams, overactive imagination, overly analytical, blocked intuition, needing everything spelled out explicitly, not being able to read between the lines, difficulty with general understanding, diminished mental acuity, cluelessness

Third Eye Chakra Stones: Heal with purple or indigo stones such as amethyst, labradorite, tanzanite, iolite, moonstone, and lepidolite

Crown Chakra Issues: Feeling superior to others, feeling more connected to the Divine than anyone else, holier-than-thou, very dreamy and not grounded, spacing out and just staring into space for a time, difficulty connecting with deity, lacking spirituality

Crown Chakra Stones: Heal with violet or white stones such as clear quartz Herkimer diamond, diamond, selenite, white calcite, and Iceland spar

If you're suffering from one of the issues listed above, it might be time to reach for your crystals. Determine what color stone you need and gather as many of those stones as you have. Place them in a circle over the associated chakra. Visualize the issue as dark energy slowly being sucked into the crystals until there is none left in your body. Visualize the color of the stones glowing and lighting up the chakra you are working with.

Remember to cleanse the stones after you are done, unless they are citrine or kyanite. Citrine and kyanite do not absorb negative energy; instead, they destroy the negative energy they suck toward them.

Working with crystals is powerful healing magic and, as you can see, it is very versatile.

Using Crystals to Support Your Spell Continuously

If you used crystals in a spell, keep the same type of crystal on you or near you. Wearing the crystal as jewelry is perfect.

Sending or Whooshing Healing

You may have seen this on social media: someone asks for healing, and they get many responses saying "Sent" or "Whoosh." Some of the people responding may have said a prayer for the person, others may have lit a candle with little thought, and some may have done serious healing spell work before stating that they sent healing.

Use the "Sending Healing Without Any Objects Involved" method described below to "whoosh" healing to someone who requested it. Remember that magical healing should always be used in addition to, never instead of, medical care.

Sending Healing Without Any Objects Involved

You can send healing from wherever you are, even if you have absolutely no tools with you.

You will need

A place to work undisturbed

Knowledge of where the person needing healing is located compared to you, directionally (optional)

If you know where the person requesting healing is located compared to you, turn in the direction of where the person is. Lift your arms so that your fingers point in the direction of the person.

Visualize sending tendrils down to the core of the earth. Draw red energy up through your feet, up your legs, and into your heart. Visualize white or violet energy coming from the Universe, entering your body through the top of your head and meeting the red energy at your heart. As the energies reach your heart, visualize them circling deosil (sunwise) around your heart. When they blend, they turn into rainbow sparks of bright light.

Visualize this light traveling from your heart, down your arms, and out through your fingers toward the person to whom you are sending healing. Visualize that person as whole and healthy. Make sure that you continue to draw energy from the earth and the Universe. Never, ever send your own energy, as this will drain you and make you ill.

Send energy for as long as you feel is necessary. Then you can, in good conscience, say "Sent" on social media!

Sending Healing Using a Candle

Sometimes you want to send healing for a more extended period than is practical to stand and send through your hands. In that case, let a candle do the sending for you.

YOU WILL NEED

A small candle (any color, but I recommend blue or green)

Matches or a lighter

A candle holder and a safe surface to let the candle burn down on

A tool to inscribe the candle (optional, and only if the candle can be inscribed)

When choosing candle size, keep in mind that a spell candle burns for two to two-and-a-half hours and needs to be watched the entire time for safety. If you are in a hurry, use a birthday candle. Remember: never leave a burning candle alone!

When choosing candle color, blue is a good choice for healing, especially mental and emotional healing, as it is associated with the element of water. A green candle is also a good choice because the element of earth is also healing.

If you have time, inscribe the candle with the energy recipient's name. You can also inscribe it with the rod of Asclepius, if you are artistically inclined. The more you layer your magic, the stronger it will be.

Proceed as if you were sending healing without an object, but instead of sending the energy to the person directly, send the energy into the candle. Then, when you light the candle, do so with the intent that it will send the healing energy to the person for as long as it burns.

As with most candle spells, you want to burn the candle completely. A partial candle spell can wreak havoc because you're sending a partial message (and partial healing) out.

I like to post a picture of the burning candle on social media if the person asked for healing in that manner. It seems to be comforting for the person who is receiving the energy. That feeling of comfort will also aid in their recovery.

Other Examples of Healing Spells

While sending or whooshing healing may be the type of healing that is most visible on social media, there are many other ways to do healing magic. Here are some very concrete healing spells.

Sending Healing Using Dolls or Poppets

Most people recoil at the thought of creating a doll or poppet for magic. The word *poppet* conjures up images of dolls full of pins, intended to harm. There are, however, many positive uses for dolls and poppets in magic. In fact, dolls and poppets are commonly used for healing magic!

To use a doll or poppet for healing magic, select a doll or poppet that will not be used as a toy. If you prefer to make your own, you can sew a poppet or even draw one on a piece of paper. Then, think about the person you are sending healing energy to. (Remember to get consent for healing before you do your working!)

If you are sewing a poppet, put a bit of the recipient's fabric or hair inside the poppet before closing it up. Also, if you can, take a long piece of yarn and measure the person from head to toe, tying a knot to indicate their height. Then measure a leg from that knot, tying another knot to show the length of their leg. From the first knot, measure the size of their arm, again tying a knot to show that length. Put this yarn inside the poppet to connect the poppet closely to the person.

Dress your poppet or decorate it in the likeness of that person. If possible, get some hair from that person or a piece of clothing that they have worn. Rub the hair on the poppet or attach it to the poppet's head with glue or tape. If you have time, fashion a piece of clothing for the poppet from the cloth you have, or rub the fabric on the poppet and let the poppet rest on the material when you do your working.

You can use poppets for better hair growth, higher or lower libido, weight loss, general health, and any other aspect of the physical body. You can also use a poppet to banish addictions. However, do so only in conjunction with addiction treatment.

Poppet for Healing

Create a poppet to heal yourself, or create a poppet for someone else who has given you consent to do so.

You will need

A doll or poppet, decorated in the likeness of the recipient

A strong infusion of healing herbs and fruits (e.g., slices of apple, cucumber, and garlic)

Isopropyl alcohol

Appropriate healing crystals

Pen

Book of Shadows, grimoire, or magical notebook for
documentation

Prepare a quick-make liniment by boiling healing herbs or fruits
in a small amount of water, creating a very strong infusion. Then
mix this infusion with isopropyl alcohol. (This recipe is the quickie
version: a traditional liniment takes four to six weeks of steeping
the herbs in isopropyl alcohol or vodka.) Also, gather healing crystals and any other healing items that you wish to use.

When the time has come for you to do your working, focus on
the body part where the ailment originates. Rub the liniment on
that part of the poppet, then set the healing crystals on top. Visualize pulling energy up from Mother Earth through your feet and
legs, and envision energy from the Universe entering through the
top of your head. Send this healing energy through your hands to
the part of the body that requires healing.

Visualize the ailment energy as dark, and see the dark energy
get heavy and drawn to the ground by gravity. Let the dark energy
sink down through the floor and down into the ground, down to
the core of the earth for cleansing. Continue pulling clean, fresh
energy up from the earth and down from the Universe and sending
it to the poppet until you can sense no more dark energy at the
place of the ailment.

Slowly let the energy flow cease. Ground yourself, eat some
chocolate, and put the poppet away. Please remember never to do
healing *instead of* medical treatment—healing spells should always
be done in conjunction with treatment.

Healing Using Cords

For this method, you can use yarn or thread. Use a natural material that will fall apart over time. You can do this for yourself, or for someone near you who needs healing and on whom you can tie the thread.

You will need

A piece of cord, string, or yarn, nine inches if very thin, three feet if thicker

Focus on the illness you are trying to heal. Then tie nine knots into the cord, visualizing the illness being bound into the knots. Draw a banishing pentagram over each knot. Tie the string loosely over the part of the body that requires healing. The cord will continue to draw the illness into the knots, and the sickness will be banished.

Keep the string on until it falls off, then discard it by burying it.

Healing for Yourself Using a Candle

You will need

A room that you can darken and where you can work undisturbed

A table and chair

A candle and candle holder that places the flame at your eye level when seated

Matches or a lighter

For this method, set a candle on a table so that the flame will be roughly at your eye level. Light the candle, then darken the room completely. Sit and focus your eyes on the candle, never looking away.

After some time, the flame will be the only thing you can see and are aware of. Sit in this trancelike state for a moment and savor it, then visualize the flame engulfing you. There is no pain, only peace. See how the flame burns the dark energy from your ailment away and then withdraws back to the wick of the candle again. The magic is in the flame, which has burnt the energy of the ailment away, so you can extinguish the candle and use it again later. The candle requires no special handling.

This spell method can take some practice, so if you don't succeed the first time, try again.

Healing by Body Cleansing

You will need

Cleansing incense (e.g., rosemary, frankincense, or clary sage)

Matches or a lighter

Noisemaking item (e.g., drum, rattle, or spoon and pot lid)

Pen and paper

Book of Shadows, grimoire, or magical notebook for
documentation

A place to work undisturbed

The body is the home of your spirit. It is the house where your self-awareness resides. As such, you can cleanse it in a way similar to how you would cleanse a home. Gather a cleansing incense such as rosemary, frankincense, or clary sage. Also, grab a drum or a similar object for noisemaking. Then write a short incantation to remove the disease; you are going to order the illness out of you.

The incantation could be along the lines of "I am whole and hale and well. Disease BEGONE! I thee tell."

Light the incense and move it from your feet all the way up your body to the top of your head. If you have a helper, have them do the same on the back of your body. Then take the noisemaking item(s) and bang them loudly while you shout your incantation.

As you repeat the incantation and make noise, visualize the disease or emotional issue moving toward your head and leaving your body through the nostrils or mouth. It could look like a wisp of smoke or even a bird or insect.

Healing Using a Magical Mirror

YOU WILL NEED

A magical mirror

Prewritten healing incantation

Pen

Book of Shadows, grimoire, or magical notebook for
documentation

A place to work undisturbed

Place the magical mirror, mirroring surface down, on the area of the body that needs healing. Say an appropriate healing incantation over the mirror, and visualize the issue being absorbed into the mirror.

Once you remove the mirror, the mirror image disappears and takes with it everything it has absorbed.

Healing Using a Paper Spell

YOU WILL NEED

A drawing or photograph of the person to be healed

Paper and pen

Book of Shadows, grimoire, or magical notebook for
documentation

A place to work undisturbed

One of the four ways to send a paper spell out (see chapter 9)

This example is a straightforward application of a paper spell.
Draw a picture of the recipient of the healing or glue a photo of
them onto a piece of paper. Write the word *healthy* across them in
capital letters. (Alternatively, write *healthy* near them with an arrow
pointing to their picture.) While you write, picture the person as
vibrant and healthy.

Write a short incantation. It might be something like, "I cast
this spell: [name] is healthy and well, for the greatest good of all,
so mote it be." Then write the short incantation on the paper. Also
state the incantation over the paper as you send energy into it.

Use one of the four methods described in chapter 9 to cast
a paper spell. As you cast the spell, again visualize the person as
whole and healthy.

Healing Using Sympathetic Magic

Both the Law of Similarity and the Law of Contagion can be
employed in healing magic.

Using the Law of Similarity relies on finding one or more items
that somehow mimic what needs to be healed, then destroying the
item(s). Destroying the object symbolizes destroying the ailment.

Another use of the Law of Similarity is finding objects that resemble or represent health, then charging them with magical power to imbue that health into the person receiving healing.

Using the Law of Contagion for healing involves working magic on items that have been in contact with the person who needs to be healed. As the object remains forever in magical connection with the person, they will receive the healing magic.

Healing Using the Law of Similarity

When you are faced with a situation where you or someone else needs healing, the first task is to identify items that look like that ailment, or items that have other similarities. There are several examples here.

Healing Using Color as the Similarity

If the ailment is associated with a color, select a cloth of that color. For example, the color red is associated with measles, German measles, rosacea, and various other rashes, and therefore you would select a red cloth. Similarly, for hepatitis, choose a yellow fabric. For nausea, choose a green material, and so on.

If the ailment isn't associated with a specific color, look at the list of ailments related to the chakras at the beginning of this chapter. Use the appropriate color for that chakra.

If you still aren't sure what color to use, or you can't access cloths of the necessary color, you can always use a white cloth and write the name of the illness or condition on it. Visualize the ailment being in the fabric.

Once you've acquired your cloth, write an incantation if you have time to do so. Then burn the cloth while visualizing the person who needs healing as healthy and free of disease. If you have written an incantation, state it while the fabric is burning.

Healing Using Items that Look Similar

Because of the Law of Similarity, items that resemble the issue or the location of the problem are excellent for healing. For example, for heart issues, cut a heart out of paper, or use the flower from a bleeding-heart plant. For a stubbed toe, draw a foot and color one of the toes red. You get the idea.

Once you've acquired your item, write an incantation if you have time to do so. Then burn the item while visualizing the person who needs healing as healthy and free of disease. If you have written an incantation, state it while the item is burning.

Healing Using a Picture of Health

You will need

A picture or drawing of the person who requested healing, from a time when they were in good health

Pen

Book of Shadows, grimoire, or magical notebook for documentation

A healthy tree at whose base you can bury the spell

If you have a picture of the person before they became in need of healing, make a copy of it and print it out, or hand-draw a copy. You don't want to destroy the original, most likely.

In this spell, you want the person to return to that state of health. Write a healing incantation to that effect if you have time. Then, on the picture, draw a boomerang to symbolize return. Repeat the incantation and continue picturing the person healthy as you fold the paper several times; you want the paper to be small and somewhat resistant to decay. Bury the paper at the base of a healthy tree. The health of the tree further layers your magic. The spell will keep working until the paper has fully decayed.

Healing Using the Law of Contagion

This kind of spell work relies on having access to an article of clothing, hair clippings, nail clippings, or something else that has been in close contact with the person who asked for healing. (If the spell is for you, this is easy.) Surround the item(s) connected to the person with soothing and healing items. Examples are herbs and crystals that are healing for specific ailments; see the chakra list at the beginning of this chapter for guidance.

Say a healing incantation and visualize the person being well. If you have something small like hair clippings or nail clippings, put them together with the herbs and stones in a small bag while you chant the incantation. If you have something large like a shirt, put the herbs and crystals on it and fold it up while chanting; you may need to tie it so that the contents do not fall out. Put the bag or the folded item of clothing somewhere where it won't be disturbed. When the spell has done its job, you can retrieve it and recover the stones. Don't forget to cleanse the stones when you have retrieved them, unless they are citrine or kyanite.

Healing Spell Using an Onion

The onion healing spell is a folk remedy that is very misunderstood. Some tout it as physically pulling bacteria and viruses out from a person when in reality, it is a magical spell for healing. It is straightforward to perform.

YOU WILL NEED

Half an onion

In the evening, cut an onion in half and put one half of it in the room where the sick person is. Visualize the onion pulling the disease out from the person. In the morning, remove the onion and throw it out. Do not cook with it; it has done its work.

Healing by Sinking the Issue into the Earth

YOU WILL NEED

A place to work undisturbed

Something to eat and drink after you have completed the spell

Scan your body, locating the issue with your inner eye. Visualize the problem as dark energy in that place. Now, in your mind, make that dark energy very heavy so that gravity starts pulling it downward. With your mind, steer the dark energy toward one of your legs and let it sink all the way down to your foot, then out through the sole. Let it sink down through the crust of the earth, through the rocks and the underground streams, all the way down the very center, where the hot, molten rock is.

See the negative energy being burned and transformed into new, clean, fresh, and healthy energy. Pull red and healthy energy back up into your feet and up your legs, filling your entire body with health and healing—be especially careful to fill the hole left by the negative energy.

Once done, have something to eat and drink, as this can be a very powerful and therefore tiring experience.

You can also do this for someone else, once you have a bit of experience. You need to walk the person through the visualization, as this spell is most powerful if the afflicted person themselves sends the negative energy away, and you never want to pull someone else's issues into yourself.

Healing by Placing the Issue Outside of the Body on the Astral Plane

YOU WILL NEED

A place to work undisturbed

Go to your astral temple. In your mind's eye, create an object that will hold your ailment and put the object safely away from you. The object can be as simple as a ball or a cube, or it can be a more elaborate item, e.g., a chest or a lockbox. You can leave the object in your temple, but I prefer to move it somewhere outside of my sacred space in the astral. I have a little clearing in a forest where I leave objects like this; I cover them with leaves so it doesn't look messy.

As in the previous method, scan your body. Locate the issue and visualize the problem as dark energy. Now, visualize that dark energy flowing up through your body and completely exiting your body through the top of your head. See the energy make its way over to the item you have created to hold it. See it enter that object and ensure all the dark energy has entered the object. Then, seal the object in your mind's eye. You can surround it with an impenetrable layer of metal or epoxy or, if it has a lock, make sure that it is locked. Leave the item in the place that you have designated for this purpose.

When you are ready, leave the astral and return to the physical space. You can do this in one of several ways.

- When you are in the astral, there is a thin, barely visible, silver thread (aka the silver cord) tying your astral body to your physical body. Look for it; once you find it, touch it and you will find yourself back in your body.

- Experienced practitioners often just think "back," and that takes them back to the physical.

- You can wiggle your fingers and toes in the astral with the intent to also wiggle them in the physical, and that will take you back to the here and now.

- Yet another way to return to the physical that some practitioners find very helpful is to have a mental doorway or gate that leads to the astral and back again.

If you feel bothered by the ailment again, go back to where you deposited the object and add additional protection around it.

Healing with Water

Healing with water is very similar to the previous method, except it is done in the shower, letting the water do the work. As water flows over you, visualize it taking the dark energy with it, flushing it out of you, and sending it down the drain.

Chapter 16

))))●●●(((

SPELLS FOR TRANSFORMATION AND LETTING GO

S ometimes it is difficult to decide what type of spell to use for a specific purpose, as there are so many to choose from. *Is a paper spell best for this? Or a candle spell?* In situations when that choice seems confusing, it is helpful to look at what kind of spells are commonly used for specific needs. This chapter gives examples of how to use different types of spells for similar purposes.

Spells for Transformation

Many different things stand as symbols of transformation. Snakes, lobsters, and crabs shed their skin or shell and are therefore associated with change. In Greek mythology, pomegranates are a symbol of transformation based on the transformation of Kore to Persephone, Queen of the Underworld. Butterflies are also a perfect symbol of transformation, going from a caterpillar to a beautiful, winged creature. The phoenix rising from the ashes is a symbol of rebirth and transformation. A seed is a powerful symbol of transformation, going from seed to seedling to plant, flower, and fruit.

When you seek transformation, you are seeking a complete change. As always, ensure that you have answered all the "Check the Ecosystem" questions in chapter 2. A complete change may have unforeseen consequences if you have not thought it through properly.

Many spells are either for banishing something or for manifesting something; a transformation spell needs to do both. One part of the spell banishes what was, and the next part brings the manifestation of something new and better in its place. You can even break the spell entirely into two separate pieces, doing a banishing spell just before the Dark Moon and a manifestation spell on Diana's Bow. These would use the techniques already set forth in earlier chapters.

Use transformation spells to break an addiction, at the time of a divorce, or when otherwise making a significant change for the better in your life.

Paper Spell for Transformation

You will need

A place to work undisturbed

Pen and paper

Book of Shadows, grimoire, or magical notebook for
documentation

Pomegranate seed (optional)

A seed that you can plant, as well as soil and an empty pot
(optional)

Decide which symbol of change you will use in this spell. You
could draw it or use the actual item. For example, if you chose a
butterfly as your symbol of change, draw a caterpillar on the left
side of a piece of paper and a butterfly on the right side. If you chose
a pomegranate seed, use an actual pomegranate seed and wrap it
inside the paper. If you want to use a seed that you can plant, you
need to have it wrapped in your paper when you perform the spell
for it to absorb the magic. Then you can plant the seed and allow its
magic to work.

Take a piece of paper. (If you drew you symbol of change, use
the same piece of paper that has your drawing on it.) On the left-hand
side of the paper, write a word or a short sentence that describes what
you want to banish. For example: "Bad relationship," "Addiction,"
"Wrong type of profession for me," etc. Then draw an X over the
word(s), signifying that they are to be banished.

On the right-hand side of the paper, write a word or short sentence that describes what you want to manifest. For example: "Freedom," "Clean and sober," "Happiness in a job," etc. Draw an arrow
pointing from left to right between the two sides, signifying that this
is a development.

Draw energy up from the earth and down from the Universe
and let it circulate through the paper, as in previous spells. Say an
appropriate incantation as you do so. Then think back to a time
where what you want to banish was present. Feel yourself slip into
your body at that time, then feel yourself walking away from what
you are dismissing—actually turning your back and walking away.

Return to your body in the now. Then look at your timeline
to see a time when what you want to manifest is present. Slip into

your body at that time and feel the emotions of having banished the old and manifested the new. Let the feelings wash over you, as that helps power the spell. Then step back into your body in the now.

If you are using a seed, place the paper at the bottom of an empty pot, put plenty of potting soil over it, plant the seed, and add additional soil. If you have only the paper, or the paper and pomegranate seed, bury it outside or burn it. While you bury it or burn it, repeat your incantation.

Cord Magic Spell for Transformation

YOU WILL NEED

An object that represents what you intend to banish (make sure it is safe to discard)

A pair of scissors

A small object that represents what you intend to manifest

Water, a moonlit night, or cleansing incense (e.g., rosemary, clary sage, or frankincense)

A thin cord or twine

A place to work undisturbed

Find a discardable object symbolizing what you want to banish and a small object representing what you want to manifest. (If you cannot think of an object that represents what you want to banish, write a word or two on a piece of paper and fold it up; this can serve as your symbolic object to banish.) Cleanse the object that symbolizes what you want to manifest by washing it, leaving it in the moonlight for a night, or holding it in the smoke of a cleansing incense such as rosemary, clary sage, or frankincense.

Take a thin cord and wrap it around the object that symbolizes what you want to banish, then tie the object to yourself. For a moment, feel how heavy it is and how it weighs you down. Then draw up energy from the earth through your feet and from the Universe through the top of your head. Let the energy circle at your heart and go out through your hands. This time, as the energy leaves your hands, see it become energy that destroys. Visualize how it destroys what binds you. Finally, draw a banishing pentagram over the object. Say an appropriate incantation, take the scissors, and cut the cord. You are free! Discard the object.

Next, pick up the object that symbolizes what you wish to manifest. Caress it and visualize yourself at the time when the manifestation has taken place. Hold the object as you slip into your body at that time and let the feelings of happiness and maybe even triumph fill you. Bring up energy from the earth and down from the Universe and let the energy mix with all your happy feelings, then see it flow into the object. Draw an invoking pentagram over the object and say an incantation for manifestation as you do so. Then slip back into your body in the now. Carry the object with you until the spell has worked its magic.

Remember to Act in Accord.

Concave Mirror Spell for Transformation

Concave mirror spells are not the easiest to perform in practical terms, at least not with the concave mirror that I have. They are, however, very powerful. This is because an object that is close to a concave mirror is seen upright in the mirror image, whereas an object that is outside of the focal length of the mirror is seen upside down. Turning a situation upside down is a powerful transformation!

You will need

A concave mirror

An object that is not vertically symmetrical (it needs to have a defined up and down) to represent the situation you wish to change

Incantation

Pen

Book of Shadows, grimoire, or magical notebook for documentation

A candle in a color that supports your transformed state (for transformation in general, orange is a good color)

An incense that supports your transformed state (for transformation in general, pomegranate incense is a good choice)

Matches or a lighter

Start by supporting a concave mirror so that it can stand without you holding it. Pick an object that is not vertically symmetrical to symbolize the situation you wish to change. The object must have a discernible upright position so that it is easy to tell when it is upside down. Now practice moving the object from inside the mirror's focal point (upright image) to outside the mirror's focal point (inverted image). This part can be tricky, so make sure you experiment with moving the object so that the transition is relatively clean when you cast your spell.

Before beginning the spell, write an incantation to support the transformation of your situation. Light a candle in a color that helps your goal, and light an appropriate incense to layer the magic.

Once you're ready to begin, place the object in front of the mirror within the focal distance, so that the image is upright. The upright image represents your current situation. While saying your incantation, slowly move the object away from the mirror until it obscures and may fall outside the mirror image.

Bring the object back so that you can see its inverted image in the mirror. Visualize your situation as having changed to what you want it to be. Send the emotions and power you feel to that point in the future. Finish with "For the greatest good of all, so mote it be!"

Move the mirror so that the image is no longer there—don't move the object out from the view of the mirror, as that is what you do to banish things. Keep the object that symbolizes the transformation with you or on your working surface.

Changing Emotions: A Different Magical Circle

This magic circle is a very versatile spell for changing your emotions—a form of transformation. Changing how you feel about something is a powerful way to change how you act. Instead of performing self-destructive acts and getting in the way of your magic, you can work in ways that support your goals.

You will need

A few feet of unobstructed space in front of you

A place to work undisturbed

First, identify the emotion you want to do away with as well as the one you want to replace it. Then search your personal timeline for a time in your life when you felt the feeling that you want to re-establish.[7] Visualize a circle about three feet in diameter in front

---

7. If you cannot find a time where you felt what you want to feel, think about what situation would give you that feeling and use the imaginary situation instead of a previous one.

of you. Move the timeline as if it were a measuring tape so that the time when you felt the desired feeling is right inside the circle.

Step into the circle and slip into your body at that time. Be in that moment. Look around and see what you saw then, hear what you heard then, smell what you smelled then, and—most importantly—feel what you felt at the time. Let the feeling envelop you and fill you up. Then, at the height of that feeling (or when you think it might start to subside), step out of the circle and move the timeline back to the here and now.

Whenever you need a boost of that feeling, visualize the circle again, take a step forward, and let it flow over and into you. Use this technique to feel confident before a job interview or an important presentation, to feel loved instead of low, or to feel courageous when facing an adversary.

Remember, magic relies on you believing in it. The magic here is moving the power that a previous situation gave you into the here and now. (If you used a potential situation, you are moving the power that would have been given to you then and making it manifest in the here and now.)

Spells for Letting Go

Most types of spells can be crafted into a spell for letting go of what no longer serves you. What no longer serves you could be a bad habit, a lost love, or guilt over something you did in the past. Remember, the past does not define you. What you do *now* defines you.

Object-Burning Spell for Letting Go

YOU WILL NEED

A flammable object that you can part with

A cauldron or other firesafe item

Matches or a lighter

Find an object you are willing to part with; anything that burns easily works well. Don't use huge objects, as you need to be able to burn them.

Take your flammable object and cleanse it by pulling up energy from the earth and down from the Universe, sending that energy out through your hands and into the object. Then visualize your lousy habit/lost love/guilt/sorrow transferring from your hands into the object. Feel it leave you. Visualize a you that is free from whatever you are ridding yourself of. Then draw a banishing pentagram over the object.

Finally, create a fire in your cauldron or other firesafe item, or make a fire in a firepit or fireplace. Burn the object and watch as what you are getting rid of gets turned into smoke and no longer has any substance. It can no longer harm you. None of it defines you.

Jar Spell for Letting Go

YOU WILL NEED

A jar with a lid

Something to represent the person for whom the spell is cast

Something to represent what is being let go

A cleansing agent (e.g., liquid soap or dishwashing liquid)

Pen

Book of Shadows, grimoire, or magical notebook for
documentation

Make a jar spell as described in chapter 9. Add a cleansing agent
if you are banishing something like a disease, addiction, or a bad
habit. The cleansing agent can be liquid soap, which is safer than
the more traditional ammonia because ammonia can make the
bottle explode.

As you visualize what you are letting go being extinguished from
existence on this planet, bury the jar where it cannot be found.

Paper Spell for Letting Go

You will need

Pen and paper

A cauldron or other firesafe item

Matches or a lighter

Book of Shadows, grimoire, or magical notebook for
documentation

A paper-burning spell is very much like an object-burning spell.
It differs in that the paper-burning spell is usually layered with sympathetic magic through the Law of Similarity, and, if possible, the
law of contagion.

Cleanse a piece of paper the way you would for an object-burning spell. Then, on the paper, write out what you want to let go.
Again, this could be something like a bad habit, or it could be the
name of someone whom you no longer want in your life. This
spell powerfully removes anything that no longer serves you.

As you write on the paper, visualize yourself without what no longer serves you. Fold the paper two or three times. You don't fold it too many times, as that makes it difficult to burn.

Light a fire in your cauldron or other firesafe item and put the paper in the fire. As you do so, watch as what you want to rid yourself of turns into smoke, into nothing, and disappears. Visualize yourself free. So mote it be.

Chapter 17

))))●●●((((

PROTECTION SPELLS
AND WARDS

Not everyone out there adheres to the ethical rules of magic. Few practitioners have the skill to inflict actual harm on someone else, though some certainly can make life less comfortable. Common signs that someone is attacking you are headaches that don't go away with regular headache medications, constipation that no amount of fiber seems to resolve, nightmares that recur night after night, hearing sounds that are not real, feeling listless for no reason, and even seeing the person who is attacking you in your mind's eye. Psychic attacks are difficult to sustain, and as with all malevolent magic, they tend to fire back on the practitioner and thereby self-extinguish. As a result, sustained psychic attacks are not very common.

If you are adept at divination or have a friend who is, the best place to start is to find out what kind of attack you are under and, if at all possible, who is behind it. The latter is usually much harder to divine, as it is typically an accomplished misfortune-magic practitioner who creates such an attack; they would typically cloak the origin of the spell so that it is impossible to discern where it is coming from.

Negative energy can also come your way without there being someone malicious behind it. Someone who feels miserable about themselves sends off negative energy without the intention of harming others, yet you need to protect yourself from it. For simplicity, I refer to these situations as attacks as well, even though there is no intended victim.

Many of the spell types that have already been presented lend themselves well to countering attacks, e.g., creating a witch's bottle or a Thoughtform, or wearing a protective amulet. In this chapter, additional types of counterspells are presented.

Wards

Wards are spells that you place around anything you want to protect. They create a magical forcefield that the attacking force cannot penetrate.

If you spend most of your time in your house, put wards around your yard. If you feel that any attacks are only happening at night, protect the room where you sleep. Wherever you think that you are being attacked, that is where you place the wards. Whenever you place wards, visualize them creating the magical forcefield that will protect you.

Pentagrams as Wards

Pentagrams are highly protective. Draw horizontal pentagrams with the points encompassing everything you are protecting. Draw pentagrams in the air with your athame or your finger, or draw them on your doorstep and around the house with chalk.

Runes as Wards

In place of drawing pentagrams, you could draw the rune Algiz. Algiz is the elk or moose, and its horns are protective.

Gargoyles and Other Imposing Figures as Wards

Using statues of gargoyles or other figures to create fear in people is a simple form of protection. However, to strengthen the protection considerably, create a Thoughtform in the sculpture. The statue should, of course, face outward from your home or room.

Mirrors as Wards

In all four directions of your home or room, hang mirrors that face outward. This will reflect back any negative energy coming toward you. Some practitioners consider this dangerous, as you are actively practicing magic that will harm someone. Others find no fault in protecting themselves in any way possible against a magical attack.

Horseshoes as Wards

Hanging a horseshoe over the entry door to a house is generally thought to bring good luck. The opening needs to face upward or otherwise "all the luck spills out," as I was told when I was a child. Lesser known is that placing horseshoes on four walls, one in each of the four directions, protects the house and its inhabitants from negative energies and attacks. This feels quite obvious, though, as good luck is not compatible with allowing magical attacks.

Witch Balls as Wards

A witch ball is a spherical glass ball with strands of glass crisscrossing it inside. It is usually green or blue or both, though there are other colors as well. The ball should be beautiful. Any evil spirits that come toward your home will be mesmerized by its beauty. As they approach it, the ball will call them to come ever closer, and when they finally touch it, they get sucked into it and trapped by the glass web inside.

Hang the ball in a window of your home in any direction where you think a threat may come from. As you do so, say a protecting incantation, focusing on trapping any evil spirits inside the ball.

Because a witch ball sucks in spirits, you need to cleanse the ball every so often. Some witches feel it is sufficient to hang the ball somewhere the morning sun hits it, which will dissolve the spirits. I prefer to cleanse the ball occasionally. Cleansing the ball requires a unique technique because you are dealing with trapped spirits. This is an advanced practice, and you should wait until you have become adept at magic before you try it. If you are just starting as a magic practitioner, you should ask someone with more experience to help with the cleansing procedure.

Cleansing a Witch Ball

Raise energy by singing, chanting, or dancing. You need to ensure that the draft of energy will be from where you are and out through the portal that you are about to open. The draft will take the spirits with it through the portal.

Draw an invoking pentagram toward the west and say an incantation indicating that you are opening the doorway to the spirit world. Emphasize that all spirits must stay on the other side and that any evil spirits on this side must leave. Then you need to free the spirits that are trapped in the ball.

First, shake the ball so that anything stuck to the web comes free. Next, push energy into the ball. Place the ball in front of the West Gate and position both hands in front of the ball with your palms facing it. Bring energy up through your feet and down through the crown of your head, then send it out through your palms. Clearing out the spirits may take some effort, and you may need to shake the ball again. It is somewhat like detangling a knotted silver chain. After you have worked at it for a while, it just happens.

Once you feel that the ball is clear, close the portal by drawing a banishing pentagram toward the West and state the incantation that you are now closing the portal.

Cleanse the witch ball as often as you feel is necessary. A witch ball never stops working, so once you have cleansed it, go ahead and hang it up again.

Protection

Sometimes you need to clear your space before setting wards. In this section you will learn a few ways of doing so, as well as a way to cast an energetic shield of protection without using any objects or substances.

House Clearing

If you feel that something has already penetrated your home or room, or you have moved into a new abode, you will want to do a house clearing before placing wards. You need to get rid of what is there first, as depending on how you set the wards, the attacking entities may not be able to get out after you have placed the wards.

You will need

Cleansing herbs or incense (e.g., rosemary, frankincense, or clary sage)

Matches or a lighter

Something to make noise with (e.g., a drum or a lid and a spoon)

To do a house clearing, start by finding cleansing herbs or incense. Rosemary, frankincense, and clary sage are all excellent choices, as they all have clearing properties. Also, get something that makes noise. It can be a noisemaker, a lid that you bang with a spoon, a drum, or anything else that is very loud. You want to make it clear to whatever is there that you mean business.

Start at the entrance door to your home or room. Light the incense and walk deosil (sunwise) all around while shouting, "Monsters, begone! Bad spirits, begone! Negative energies, this is not your home, begone!" Alternate with "Attacking entities, begone! Anything not invited, you are not welcome here, begone! OUT, all nasties." You can make up your own words for what you need to dispel from the place.

A house clearing is most easily done with more than one person. One person can open drawers and doors, one person can hold the incense and waft the smoke into closets and drawers, one person can make noise, and all visualize the home as clear and free of anything that does not belong.

If you do this alone, first walk around and open all the drawers and doors to cabinets and closets, then walk around with the incense while shouting and visualizing the home as being free of anything that should not be there. Finally, walk around with the noisemaker while shouting and visualizing.

You can end by sprinkling salt around the inside or outside perimeter of the house, if you can do so safely, without risking damage to the floors or vegetation. However, since this is rarely possible, you can instead place small containers of salt in each room.

While this is called a house clearing, it can be used anywhere. For example, if you have a business that is not doing well, do a clearing of the office to allow the company to start fresh. Likewise, if you keep livestock of any kind and they are not producing, clear the barn or the henhouse.

Salt for Protection

YOU WILL NEED

Salt

Plastic bag

Something to carry the plastic bag in

In addition to using salt around your house or room, you can carry salt on you for protection. Salt clears all negative energies, including any sort of spell attacking you. Put some salt in a plastic bag, then put the plastic bag in a silk bag or similar to protect it. The bag will keep you safe from any magical attack for as long as you carry it.

Chapter 17

Protecting Yourself with an Energetic Bubble Shield

You will need

Only yourself

It is always ethical to protect yourself. Take a deep breath and visualize sending tendrils from your feet deep down into the center of the earth. Draw up red, clean energy through the tendrils, up through your legs, and up to your perineum. Now let the energy rise to just below your navel. See the energy turn orange before it rises to your solar plexus area and turns yellow. It is as if you have a bright yellow light emanating from your solar plexus. Let this light envelope you and form an oval bubble around you. Make the bubble impenetrable. The bubble protects you against anything that is coming at you.

Now relax the bubble so that it is semipermeable. Make sure it protects against negative energies but allows in positive energy. Your bubble may be yellow or a different color. Practice calling up this shield so that you 1) can pull it up in a split second, completely hardened, when needed, and 2) can keep it up, semipermeable, whenever you are out and about.

Always keep your bubble shield fully hardened around any car that you drive or ride in, and make sure it is around the entire airplane when you fly.

Chapter 18

))))●●(((

SPELLS FOR LOVE AND BEAUTY

There are endless variations on love and beauty spells available in print and online; I hesitated about whether to include examples. I decided to include just a couple because these examples put into practice the principles you have learned in earlier chapters. The spell to get married shows you how to use a poppet for magic other than healing. The spell for beauty within and without puts charging an object with magic into practice.

Spell for Love

Before heading into any love spell, please make sure that you remember and understand the ethics of such magic. Do not interfere with someone else's free will.

Poppet Spell to Find a Spouse and Get Married

This spell is a spell to find a spouse, not to marry a particular person.

You will need

A poppet that looks like you, to represent you

A nondescript poppet, to represent your future spouse

A poppet-sized wedding venue

Flowers and herbs that attract love (e.g., roses, basil, and saffron)

An incantation stating that you are happily married

Pen

Book of Shadows, grimoire, or magical notebook for documentation

A space where you can work undisturbed

Create two poppets, one to represent you and one to represent your future spouse. Make the one that represents you look as much like you as possible. Add some strands of your hair to it. Make the one that represents your future spouse very nondescript—you don't want the magic to accidentally exclude a perfect match because they have a different hair color than your poppet did.

Set up a wedding venue of the type you would like to get married in, but make it an appropriate size for the poppets. Decorate the space with flowers and herbs that attract love, such as rose, basil, and saffron. Perform a wedding ceremony for the poppets, with the intent that you are getting married. End the ceremony with an incantation stating that you are happily married.

Keep the poppets until after you have found your match and gotten married. After that, they have done their magic and can be discarded. Alternatively, you might find it romantic to keep them and bring them out for anniversaries.

Spell for Beauty

Perhaps the most famous magic for beauty is to get up early on Beltane (May 1) and wash one's face with the morning dew. I reference this practice in the incantation for the following spell.

Spell for Beauty Within and Without

Cast the spell presented here if you want to have your inner beauty shine and reflect in your outer beauty. As within, so without!

If at all possible, have the incantation and spell memorized. If you have to read from a paper, then do so, but keep in mind that it is harder to raise power while reading.

You WILL NEED

A piece of rose quartz

Space to move around in a circle

A place where you can work undisturbed

Invite the goddess Aphrodite, goddess of love and beauty, into your space by using the following incantation:

))))●●●(((

I call upon thee, lovely Aphrodite, glorious bringer of beauty and sensuality, daughter of Uranus, and of Zeus and Dione.

No tricksters or traitors are welcome here, only the true soul and spirit of Lady Aphrodite.

Aphrodite, lady of pleasure and joy, born of the sea-foam, also known as Acidalia, Cytherea, and Cerigo,

By red-colored rose, by scallop shells, and by the grace of the dove, I invite thee, Lady Aphrodite, to attend and bless my space so that I may learn and grow in love and beauty.

Hail and welcome, Lady Aphrodite!

)))❨●●●❩(((

Now it is time to cast your spell. The spell will supercharge the rose quartz crystal. Start moving clockwise in your space while holding the rose quartz. Say:

)))❨●●●❩(((

Like Aphrodite
I am gorgeous and fetching and fine.
I'm delightful and truly divine.
I am subtly seductive and warm,
And my shape is a beautiful form.
When I wish, I am smoldering hot.
I am polished yet know what I've got!
I'm alluring, exquisite, refined,
And it's thus I am seen by mankind.
Divine beauty inside doth shine through
Reflects, daily, Beltane morning dew.

)))❨●●●❩(((

Repeat this spell three times. Each time you say it, speak faster and louder. Move faster each time, and raise your hands higher and higher as you go. At the end of the third repetition, shout:

))))●●●(((C

OH YES!!!

So mote it be!

))))●●●(((C

Send the spell out into the Universe and into the rose quartz to manifest. Then sit down and relax.

Thank Aphrodite before saying farewell to her.

Whenever you need that sense of being radiantly beautiful, inside and out, hold your rose quartz—the magic is in it.

Conclusion

))))●●●(((

BEFORE YOU GO

You now possess all the tools you need to make your life successful with the help of magic. The difference between succeeding and being stuck in the status quo is practicing what you have learned. As you practice, you will find that your understanding of how to execute a spell increases, and you will become increasingly adept at manifesting your desires.

You need to be motivated to manifest your goal. When you are, practicing becomes second nature. Motivation also plays into the magic itself. When you are motivated, your emotions are more potent, and the energy you build is more powerful as you perform the spell. If you find that you are not motivated enough to manifest your goal, you very likely have selected a goal that you do not truly and honestly desire. Find a different one: one that really causes you to do the work joyfully. You need to be dedicated to that work.

Acting in accord is a necessary step of the magic, and putting one foot in front of the other requires dedication to your goal. If you find your enthusiasm waning, even if it was great initially, it is time to reassess whether this is a goal you still really want. If you find that your drive and stamina are lacking, you may need to first set "drive and energy" as your goal; work to achieve that goal so you can apply the results to your next goal.

You need to be adaptable. If something goes awry, assess the new situation quickly and grasp how you need to change course. You need to accept and adapt to change so that your work can continue. Flexibility is the name of the game. A witch is resourceful! You need to be open to learning new skills and new approaches when the situation changes. Be resilient enough to manage the temporary setback. You need to have an optimistic and positive outlook—always. Find the reasons why the new approach will work! Find new energy and enthusiasm from the challenges and complexities, and stay confident that you will succeed. When there are issues, focus on finding solutions, and remember that you are responsible for your own reality. Don't look for scapegoats. Sometimes, when you encounter an issue, you need to stop. If you keep moving forward, some problems will cause you to waste time and resources when instead you should have paused and reassessed.

At times, you may need to take risks to get your goal to manifest. Always be on the lookout for ways that you can shorten the Acting in Accord worklist. If there is risk associated with the shortcut, weigh the risks and the benefits. Taking no risks at all usually results in a snail's-pace approach.

If you are seemingly going nowhere and believe that you are doing all the Acting in Accord steps, analyze the actions you have written down. Ensure that each step is clear and specific so that you know exactly what to do. Ensure that the steps are not written as goals in themselves; you need to have the steps be actual, executable actions. Make sure that you understand why each step is necessary. It is easy to lose enthusiasm when doing something you don't understand the purpose of. Make sure that the steps call out when you should do each of them; this way, you can hold yourself accountable to a schedule. You can even add little rewards for yourself here and there in the steps. For example, once you have done steps one, two, and three, add a step four: "Celebrate this milestone." Maybe you get ice cream from the ice cream parlor!

As with most everything, it is the effort you put in that will determine the outcome. If your spells are consistently brief and put together without thought, you may find that you have less success than you had hoped for. Practice makes perfect. The more you practice, the more you will accomplish. Spell working is second nature for most successful practitioners because practice has caused all aspects of spell working to be an integral part of who they are. Don't give up if your first spell does not work. Check all aspects of the magic: whether the eco-system is there for the goal to manifest, what correspondences you used, the wording of the incantation, the timing of casting the spell, and whether you were raising the energy needed. Check that you took all the steps to Act in Accord. Tweak anything that needs to be tweaked and try again. If, after three tries, it still does not manifest, that is telling you something: your goal is not in balance with the Universe. No matter how hard you try, your magic will not be able to upset the balance. The Laws of Nature still apply. Gravity still exists. The Wheel of the Year will turn, and winter will come after fall. Magic is not miracles. Magic is making the possible probable. When your goal fails to manifest three times, you need to sit down and understand why the goal you set is not in tune with the rest of the Universe. Doing so is tough and can be a hard lesson to learn. Don't despair, and don't give up. Once you understand why your goal upsets the balance, you can decide on a goal that meets your needs *and* is in tune with the Universe.

As your experience grows, you will find that knowing whether a goal is in balance with the Universe becomes nearly automatic. With time, you will not chase impossible dreams that cannot materialize. As you become more adept at setting your intent so it doesn't upset the balance of the Universe, you will find that more and more of your spells manifest what you wish for. This evolution is part of the normal development of a practitioner. In other words, if your first spell fails, don't worry! In a short time, you will be creating spells that work—every single one of them!

Appendix

))))●●●●(((((

SPELL INGREDIENTS

This appendix contains spells listed by number of ingredients. This way, if you're interested in doing a spell but don't have access to many ingredients, you have some idea of where to begin.

Spells in This Book That Require No Ingredients

Chapter 6: Spell Using Only the Elements

Chapter 12: Energetic-Only Thoughtform

Chapter 14: Anytime Spell for Clearing and Protection

Chapter 14: Spell for Success in Something That You Are Just About to Do

Chapter 14: Protection Against Anything Coming at You

Chapter 15: Healing by Placing the Issue Outside of the Body on the Astral Plane

Chapter 15: Sending Healing Without Any Objects Involved

Chapter 16: Changing Emotions: A Different Magical Circle

Chapter 17: Protecting Yourself with an Energetic Bubble Shield

Spells in This Book That Require One Ingredient

Chapter 4: Rune Prosperity Spell
  1. Access to the rune chart in this chapter, unless you already know the meaning of each runestave

Chapter 9: Cord Magic to Protect Against Theft
  1. Nine-inch piece of string or thin yarn

Chapter 14: Morning Spell for a Good Day
  1. A food or beverage that you consume in the morning

Chapter 15: Healing by Sinking the Issue into the Earth
  1. Something to eat and drink after you have completed the spell

Chapter 15: Healing Spell Using an Onion
  1. Half an onion

Chapter 15: Healing Using Cords
  1. A piece of cord, string, or yarn, nine inches if very thin, three feet if thicker

Chapter 18: Spell for Beauty Within and Without

    1. A piece of rose quartz

Spells in This Book That Require Three Ingredients

Chapter 9: Moon Water to Fortify Spells

    1. Water, preferably rainwater or water from a stream or body of water, but tap water works

    2. A jar with a lid

    3. A night with a full moon

Chapter 9: Paper Spell

    1. Pen

    2. Paper or birch bark

    3. Book of Shadows, grimoire, or magical notebook for documentation

Chapter 9: Send Healing Using Candle Magic

    1. A candle in an appropriate color for healing (e.g., blue)

    2. Oil for anointing the candle

    3. Matches or a lighter

Chapter 9: Simple Braided Spell

    1. Three cords, either nine-inch cords or cords that are three feet or nine feet long

    2. Pen

    3. Book of Shadows, grimoire, or magical notebook for documentation

Chapter 15: Healing for Yourself Using a Candle
1. A table and chair

2. A candle and candle holder that places the flame at your eye level when seated

3. Matches or a lighter

Chapter 16: Object-Burning Spell for Letting Go
1. A flammable object that you can part with

2. A cauldron or other firesafe item

3. Matches or a lighter

Chapter 17: House Clearing
1. Cleansing herbs or incense (e.g., rosemary, frankincense, or clary sage)

2. Matches or a lighter

3. Something to make noise with (e.g., a drum or a lid and a spoon)

Chapter 17: Salt for Protection
1. Salt

2. Plastic bag

3. Something to carry the plastic bag in

Spells in This Book That Require Four Ingredients

Chapter 2: Supper for Prosperity Using Religious Magic
1. A table that can be set for a meal

2. An as-elegant-as-possible table setting for deity

3. Foods that are known to be favored by the god or goddess you have chosen to work with

4. A table setting and a meal for yourself, if you wish

Chapter 9: Mirror Spell for Confidence

1. A magical mirror

2. Incantation

3. Pen

4. Book of Shadows, grimoire, or magical notebook for documentation

Chapter 9: Witch's Ladder

1. A three-foot cord

2. Pen

3. Book of Shadows, grimoire, or magical notebook for documentation

4. Items that support your goal, which will be tied into the ladder (optional)

Chapter 15: Sending Healing Using a Candle

1. A small candle (any color, but I recommend blue or green)

2. Matches or a lighter

3. A candle holder and a safe surface to let the candle burn down on

4. A tool to inscribe the candle (optional, and only if the candle can be inscribed)

Chapter 15: Healing Using a Magical Mirror

1. A magical mirror

2. Prewritten healing incantation

3. Pen

4. Book of Shadows, grimoire, or magical notebook for documentation

Chapter 15: Healing Using a Paper Spell

1. A drawing or photograph of the person to be healed

2. Paper and pen

3. Book of Shadows, grimoire, or magical notebook for documentation

4. One of the four ways to send a paper spell out (see chapter 9)

Chapter 15: Healing Using a Picture of Health

1. A picture or drawing of the person who requested healing, from a time when they were in good health

2. Pen

3. Book of Shadows, grimoire, or magical notebook for documentation

4. A healthy tree at whose base you can bury the spell

Chapter 16: Paper Spell for Letting Go

1. Pen and paper

2. A cauldron or other firesafe item

3. Matches or a lighter

4. Book of Shadows, grimoire, or magical notebook for documentation

Chapter 16: Paper Spell for Transformation

    1. Pen and paper

    2. Book of Shadows, grimoire, or magical notebook for documentation

    3. Pomegranate seed (optional)

    4. A seed that you can plant, as well as soil and an empty pot (optional)

Spells in This Book That Require Five Ingredients

Chapter 9: Magical Holy Water

    1. Water, preferably moon water

    2. A cauldron or chalice

    3. Salt

    4. A bottle to store the water in

    5. An athame (optional)

Chapter 12: Prodeety: A Thoughtform for PROtection from Dogs EntEring The Yard

    1. Bowl of soil

    2. Bowl with drops of corresponding oil in a carrier oil

    3. Corresponding incense

    4. Matches or a lighter

    5. Corresponding potion

Chapter 15: Healing by Body Cleansing

    1. Cleansing incense (e.g., rosemary, frankincense, or clary sage)

    2. Matches or a lighter

3. Noisemaking item (e.g., drum, rattle, or spoon and pot lid)

4. Pen and paper

5. Book of Shadows, grimoire, or magical notebook for documentation

Chapter 16: Cord Magic Spell for Transformation

1. An object that represents what you intend to banish (make sure it is safe to discard)

2. A pair of scissors

3. A small object that represents what you intend to manifest

4. Water, a moonlit night, or cleansing incense (e.g., rosemary, clary sage, or frankincense)

5. A thin cord or twine

Spells in This Book That Require Six Ingredients

Chapter 9: Mirror Spell for Self-Love

1. A magical mirror

2. Two candles

3. Matches or a lighter

4. A table to sit at

5. Pen

6. Paper

Chapter 13: Seed Spell

1. Pen

2. Paper

3. Book of Shadows, grimoire, or magical notebook for documentation

4. Flowerpot

5. Potting soil

6. Seed of a plant that you already know how to grow

Chapter 15: Poppet for Healing

1. A doll or poppet, decorated in the likeness of the recipient

2. A strong infusion of healing herbs and fruits (e.g., slices of apple, cucumber, and garlic)

3. Isopropyl alcohol

4. Appropriate healing crystals

5. Pen

6. Book of Shadows, grimoire, or magical notebook for documentation

Chapter 16: Jar Spell for Letting Go

1. A jar with a lid

2. Something to represent the person for whom the spell is cast

3. Something to represent what is being let go

4. A cleansing agent (e.g., liquid soap or dishwashing liquid)

5. Pen

6. Book of Shadows, grimoire, or magical notebook for documentation

Spells in This Book That Require Seven Ingredients

Chapter 18: Poppet Spell to Find a Spouse and Get Married

1. A poppet that looks like you, to represent you

2. A nondescript poppet, to represent your future spouse

3. A poppet-sized wedding venue

4. Flowers and herbs that attract love (e.g., roses, basil, and saffron)

5. An incantation stating that you are happily married

6. Pen

7. Book of Shadows, grimoire, or magical notebook for documentation

Spells in This Book That Require Eight Ingredients

Chapter 9: Ending Love Jar

1. A glass jar with a lid

2. A place to bury the jar

3. Paper

4. Pen

5. A bitter liquid (e.g., overly strong tea or burned coffee)

6. Vinegar

7. Prewritten incantation

8. Book of Shadows, grimoire, or magical notebook for documentation

Chapter 9: Witch's Bottle

1. A glass jar with a lid

2. A place to hide the jar

3. Something from the person to be protected (e.g., hair or nail clippings or urine)

4. Nails and pins

5. Prewritten protection incantation

6. Pen

7. Book of Shadows, grimoire, or magical notebook for documentation

8. Rosemary or frankincense essential oil (optional)

Chapter 16: Concave Mirror Spell for Transformation

1. A concave mirror

2. An object that is not vertically symmetrical (it needs to have a defined up and down) to represent the situation you wish to change

3. Incantation

4. Pen

5. Book of Shadows, grimoire, or magical notebook for documentation

6. A candle in a color to support that supports your transformed state (for transformation in general, orange is a good color)

7. An incense that supports your transformed state (for transformation in general, pomegranate incense is a good choice)

8. Matches or a lighter

Spells in This Book That Require Nine Ingredients

Chapter 9: Honey Jar Spell

1. A glass jar with a lid

2. A place to bury the jar

3. Paper or birch bark to write on

4. Pen

5. Book of Shadows, grimoire, or magical notebook for documentation

6. A sweetener (e.g., honey, syrup, or sugar water)

7. Beeswax

8. Prewritten love incantation (optional)

9. Symbols of sweetness (optional)

Spells in This Book That Require Ten or More Ingredients

Chapter 2: Spell for Prosperity Using Religious Magic

1. A photo or drawing of a messy part of your home: dirty dishes, an unmade bed, or similar

2. A picture or statue of Kamadhenu, the Hindu "cow of plenty," or another cow

3. A photograph or drawing of the messy part of your home after you have cleaned it up (done the dishes, made the bed, etc.) with the picture or statue of Kamadhenu or cow visible in the clean space

4. A statue, picture, drawing, or other representation of the goddess Lakshmi

5. A brazier or other way of burning one of the pictures

6. Cloth to present to the representation of Lakshmi

7. A table or horizontal surface to work on

8. High-percentage isopropyl alcohol

9. Epsom salt

10. Long matches

To prepare yourself and your space, you need:

1. Oils, herbs, or scented candles that connect you with deity and that support prosperity. Cinnamon, basil, and cloves are suggested

2. If possible, garments for yourself that are pink and gold, or garments with gold accents

3. Sweet-smelling incense, e.g., fruit or rose

4. If available, a lotus-shaped candle holder

5. A clean cloth for your table surface

Chapter 9: Paper Spell for Successful Vending at an Event

1. Paper

2. Pen

3. Marjoram

4. Nutmeg

5. Cumin

6. A coin, preferably the largest denomination in the currency used wherever the event is held

7. Knowledge of how to draw the symbol for the planet Mercury

8. Knowledge of how to draw the symbol for the zodiac sign Taurus

9. An envelope

10. A place to burn or bury the envelope

Chapter 9: Spell Bag

1. A piece of leather or material; chamois is popular for spell bags

2. Thread or string to close the bag with

3. Gemstones or other small objects that correspond with your intent

4. Herbs that support your intent

5. Incense that supports your intent

6. Matches or a lighter

7. Pen

8. Pentacle plate or a piece of paper with a pentacle drawn on it

9. Strainer

10. Body fluid, liquor, or perfume

11. Book of Shadows, grimoire, or magical notebook for documentation

Chapter 12: Object-Based Thoughtform

1. An object to hold the Thoughtform

2. Elemental incantations

3. A substance that symbolizes earth (e.g., soil)

4. An oil that supports your intent

5. A potion/tea made with herbs that support the intent of the Thoughtform

6. An incense that supports the intent

7. Matches or a lighter

8. Tributes that support your intent, to be given to the Thoughtform

9. Pen

10. Book of Shadows, grimoire, or magical notebook for documentation

Chapter 12: Creating a Coyote Thoughtform for Protection
1. No-bake or oven-bake clay for earth

2. Dragon's blood essential oil for fire

3. A protective potion for water (e.g., an infusion made from bay leaf, caraway seeds, cloves, and garlic)

4. A protective incense for air (e.g., frankincense fortified with myrrh)

5. Matches or a lighter

6. Pentagram

7. Tiger's eye crystal

8. Wooden figa

9. Silver bracelet

10. Acorn

11. Black opal

Chapter 12: Peace in a Candle
1. A candleholder

2. A candle as a tribute

3. Matches or a lighter

4. Dry soil

5. Corresponding oil

6. Corresponding potion / tea

7. Corresponding incense

8. Wiccan Rede (can be found online)

9. A piece of amethyst

10. A piece of hematite

GLOSSARY

There are some terms in this book with which you may not be familiar. They are explained here.

banishing: To get rid of, remove, or allow to leave.

Book of Shadows: Witches often keep a document called the Book of Shadows where they collect rituals and other information of importance, e.g., correspondences for the elements.

brazier: A fireproof container in which you can light a fire for use during spell workings. It needs to be set on a heatproof surface.

cauldron: Can hold water, fire, soil and flowers, and incense. It is therefore whole and holy, representing all the elements. Secondarily, the cauldron also represents water and is sometimes used as the water tool for a group working together.

censer: A container in which to burn incense.

centering: To focus inward and to become still. To calm emotions. It is usually done in conjunction with grounding.

charcoal round or charcoal tablet: Specifically made for burning dried herbs or resin incense. In the US, most are quick lighting, meaning that once one side is lit, the entire tablet will light within ten minutes or so. To burn, place the incense in a *censer* or incense burner on a heatproof surface.

clairaudience: The ability to hear what your two ears cannot hear. The ability to hear spirits or to listen to sounds that occur far away.

clairvoyance: The ability to see what your two eyes cannot see. The ability to see spirits or occurrences that take place far away.

divination: To discern the answer to a question through tarot, magic mirror, runes, or other magical means. It can be a way of channeling the voice of deity.

epithet: A word that describes the characteristics of a deity or an aspect of a deity.

grimoire: A book containing a collection of spells and instructions for the creation of magical objects.

grounding: To get rid of excess nervous energy and draw up fresh, calm energy from Mother Earth.

incantation: The words that, in a condensed format, define the intent of a spell. Sometimes written with a meter and in rhyme.

incense: Commonly lit during magical workings. A symbol of air. Can be used to consecrate sacred space with the element of air. Can be used to set the mood for spell work.

pentagram: Symbolic of the four elements (earth, fire, water, and air), with the fifth point, the upward point, symbolizing Spirit. Many witches wear a necklace with an encircled pentagram pendant to connect with the elements and Spirit throughout the day. A symbol of earth.

portal: A doorway to another realm. Can be to an elemental realm or to the world of spirits, for example.

psychopomp: Someone who guides the souls of the dead to their final destination.

salt: Represents the element of earth. Will cleanse any object of all energies so that the object can be recharged. Use with caution, as salt will erase desired energies along with everything else.

BIBLIOGRAPHY

Aswynn, Freya. *Northern Mysteries and Magick: Runes & Feminine Powers*. Woodbury, MN: Llewellyn Publications, 2009.

Burk, Kevin. *Astrology: Understanding the Birth Chart*. St. Paul, MN: Llewellyn Publications, 2003.

Conway, D. J. *Moon Magick: Myth & Magic, Crafts & Recipes, Rituals & Spells*. St. Paul, MN: Llewellyn Publications, 2002.

Cunningham, Scott. *Magical Herbalism: The Secret Craft of the Wise*. St. Paul, MN: Llewellyn Publications, 2003.

———. *Cunningham's Encyclopedia of Magical Herbs*. Woodbury, MN: Llewellyn Publications, 2016.

Farrar, Stewart, and Janet Farrar. *A Witches' Bible: The Complete Witches' Handbook*. Custer, WA: Phoenix Publishing, 1984.

Bibliography

Frater, U.:D.: *Practical Sigil Magic: Creating Personal Symbols for Success*. Woodbury, MN: Llewellyn Publications, 2012.

Frazer, James George. *The Golden Bough*. London: Macmillan, 1966.

Gaynor, Frank, Edwin Radford, Mona A. Radford, and Harry E. Wedeck. *The Witchcraft Collection Volume Two: Dictionary of Mysticism, Encyclopedia of Superstitions, and Dictionary of Magic*. New York: Philosophical Library, 2019.

Hall, Manly Palmer. *The Secret Teachings of All Ages*. Radford, VA: Wilder Publications, 2007.

Hawke, Elen. *Praise to the Moon: Magic & Myth of the Lunar Cycle*. St. Paul, MN: Llewellyn Publications, 2002.

Hogendorn, Jan, and Marion Johnson. *The Shell Money of the Slave Trade*. Cambridge, UK: Cambridge University Press, 2003.

LaVeau, Belladonna. *Awakening Spirit: WISE Seminary, First Year Certification for Wiccan Clergy*. Victoria, BC, Canada: Trafford Publishing, 2003.

Nichols, Mike. *Re-Thinking the Watchtowers: 13 Reasons Air Should Be in the North*. Self-published, 1989. https://www.sacred-texts.com/bos/bos089.htm.

"Of Religion by Discernment." In *Bhagavad Gita*. Accessed March 6, 2022. https://www.sacred-texts.com/hin/gita/bg07.htm.

"The Pentagram in Depth." SymbolDictionary.net. Accessed September 16, 2021. http://symboldictionary.net/?p=1893.

Bibliography

Sams, Jamie, and David Carson. *Medicine Cards: The Discovery of Power through the Ways of Animals*. New York: St. Martin's Press, 1999.

Willis, Tony. *Discover Runes: Understanding and Using the Power of Runes*. New York: Sterling Pub Co, 1993.